T l

of

DECISION

A Guide to
Making Good Choices
for Your Life

Marla.

Esther 4:14

NTillotson

Dr. Nathan Tillotson

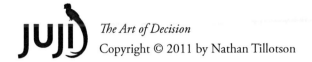

The Art of Decision
Copyright © 2011 by Nathan Tillotson

Editorial services provided by Snapdragon Group℠ Tulsa, OK, USA
Artwork and diagrams by Jason David Kingsley
Photography by Rebekah Elena

Printed in the USA

I would like to dedicate this book
to my wife Libby
and my three daughters:
Katherine, Victoria, and Rebekah.
I love you with all my heart.
And also to the Holy Spirit,
who is my constant friend, teacher, counselor, and strength.

CONTENTS

PREFACE

In the fall of 2000, I was serving on active duty as an army physician. A couple I knew made a poor decision that caused them major problems, and it inspired me to see what the Bible had to say about the decision-making process.

What I saw almost immediately was that one bad decision can have devastating consequences. Biblical characters who started out living for God had major setbacks because of the poor choices they made. King Solomon, considered the wisest man who ever lived, is a good example. Solomon started off strong for God, but when he chose to marry foreign women, his heart was turned toward the idolatry his wives practiced and away from God. As a result, his kingdom was divided.

"If Solomon, the wisest man who ever lived, stumbled at the end of his life," I asked God, "how could I or anyone else hope to make good decisions that would help us stay strong throughout our lives?" The Lord replied, "I will teach you."

Over the next two years I memorized the book of Proverbs. I wanted to get inside Solomon's head and see decision making through his eyes. As I familiarized myself with the 915 verses laid out before me like jigsaw puzzle pieces, I asked God to show me the big picture. After all, this puzzle had no puzzle box for reference. Finally God helped me see what I was looking for.

 The foundational scriptures that pulled everything together leaped off the page at me: "The ear that hears the rebukes of life will abide among the wise. He who disdains instruction despises his own soul, but he who heeds rebuke gets understanding. The fear of the LORD is the instruction of wisdom, and before honor is humility" (Proverbs 15:31–33).

The next three years of my life were focused on studying the decision-making principles in that passage. During that time, the Lord showed me how to organize those principles into a seven-step diagram.

It didn't occur to me at first to put all this into book form. Deep down, though, I knew God had given me something that needed to be shared and the idea took shape. By January of 2006, writing a book on decision making had gone from something I *could* do to something I *should* do. Soon after, the Lord gave me a story that illustrated the decision-making principles I had learned, and writing the book became something I *must* do. I began writing *The Art of Decision* in August of 2006. It would be finished four years later, a decade after I started the project.

HEBREW *Chokmah* |khok-maw'|: Wisdom

The ability to make good decisions.

INTRODUCTION

*Wisdom and knowledge will be the stability of
your times.*—Isaiah 33:6

The Art of Decision is the culmination of years of studying the
book of Proverbs. It contains the decision-making genius of Solomon condensed into seven practical steps. Learning the seven
steps is simple, while mastering them requires practice, time,
and effort. Invest in them, however, and you will see greater
success in every area of your life. In Proverbs 4:7–9, Solomon
himself said this: "Wisdom is the principal thing; therefore get
wisdom. And in all your getting, get understanding. Exalt her,
and she will promote you; she will bring you honor when you
embrace her. She will place on your head an ornament of grace;
a crown of glory she will deliver to you."

As you read through these pages, you will see that three
plagues were unleashed on mankind after the fall of Adam and
Eve. The first two plagues were sin and disease. Jesus paid the
price for these two at the cross on our behalf. We receive His
salvation and healing by faith.

A third, external plague unleashed on mankind is deception, which leads to poor decision making. It is easy to see the devastation it has caused throughout the centuries. Scripture tells us that this is a plague every person must deal with and that it will intensify in the last days. "The Spirit expressly says that in latter times some will depart from the faith, giving heed to deceiving spirits and doctrines of demons" (1 Timothy 4:1).

As a Christian physician, I took it upon myself to find a scriptural antidote to help combat this third plague. I knew I was on the right track when I read Isaiah 59:19, which says: "When the enemy comes in like a flood, the Spirit of the LORD will lift up a standard against him."

The principles in *The Art of Decision* will work for you in all areas of life. My prayer is that it will be a travel bag you can take with you wherever you go. Get ready to embark on your own decision-making adventure!

We are His workmanship, created in Christ Jesus for good works, which God prepared beforehand that we should walk in them.—Ephesians 2:10

CHAPTER 1

Five Reasons for Gaining Wisdom

The list of reasons to seek wisdom is long. Five of those reasons are included in this chapter. Note that the terms "wisdom" and "good decision making" are used interchangeably.

REASON #1: GOD HAS A PLAN FOR YOUR LIFE.

Even before He set the foundations of the world in place, God formulated a great plan for your life. Jeremiah 29:11 (NLT) says, "I know the plans I have for you," says the LORD. "They are plans for good and not for disaster, to give you a future and a hope." It is God's will for you to be strong and carry out His great plan for you. Knowing your God is the first step to doing that.

REASON #2: WISDOM, ALONG WITH FAITH,
IS REQUIRED TO FULFILL GOD'S PLAN.

Every life is based on faith in something or someone. Some people put their faith in a philosophy, an organization, a person, or perhaps themselves. As Christians, our lives are based on faith in Jesus Christ as our Savior and the Bible, the instruction manual He left for us.

- "The just shall live by (his) *faith*" (Habakkuk 2:4; Romans 1:17; and Galatians 3:11).

- "We walk by *faith*, not by sight" (2 Corinthians 5:7).

Hebrews 12:2 says Jesus is the *author and finisher of our faith*. While we are to *live* and *walk* by faith in God, we are to be directed by wisdom from God. James 1:5 says, *"If any of you lacks wisdom, let him ask of God, who gives to all liberally and without reproach, and it will be given to him."*

Notice that it says God gives wisdom to all liberally. God does not play favorites. Every person is invited to receive wisdom

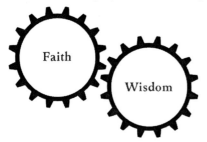

from God liberally, which means in abundance. Faith and wisdom work in harmony, like gears.

What is the difference between the two?

Faith answers the question of *what* to believe.

Wisdom answers the question of *how* to get what you believe.

Hebrews 11:1 defines faith this way: "Faith is the substance of things hoped for, the evidence of things not seen." Romans 10:17 teaches us how to grow in faith: "So then faith comes by hearing, and hearing by the word of God." Just as Hebrews 11:1 teaches us what faith is and Romans 10:17 teaches us how to grow in faith, Proverbs 15:31–33 tells us how to grow in wisdom. "The ear that hears the rebukes of life will abide among the wise. He who disdains instruction despises his own soul, but he who heeds rebuke gets understanding. The fear of the LORD is the instruction of wisdom, and before honor is humility"

We can see from these scriptures that knowing what wisdom is and how to grow in wisdom is just as important as knowing what faith is and how to grow in faith.

- Faith *sees* and *believes* in the end result.

- Wisdom *enables* us to obtain what we are seeing and believing God for.

- Both faith and wisdom come from God.

James 2:20 tells us that faith without works is dead. If wisdom gives faith direction, then. . . *faith without wisdom is directionless.*

Have you ever seen a loose cannon or an arrow without feathers? They can be easily misdirected and cause unintended damage. A person can have great faith, but if that person lacks the wisdom to go along with it, they can go astray. This is why even strong Christians can make big mistakes. This is why it is important to have both faith and wisdom operating in your life.

No matter what you are believing God for, wisdom will help you get there. Perhaps you are believing for a better marriage, a new career, a more efficient business, improved leadership skills, or more impactful ministry. Wisdom will *enable* you to get from where you are to where God wants you to be. Faith sees and believes. Wisdom enables. People sometimes get frustrated and quit because they are exercising their faith but nothing happens. The problem may be a lack of wisdom. Because wisdom gives faith direction.

REASON #3: WISDOM WORKS IN ALL CIRCUMSTANCES.

Whether you realize it or not, your life consists of making one decision after another. The minute you wake up in the morning, you make the decision to press the snooze button and go back to sleep or get up and greet the day. From there you must decide to shower or not to shower and what you will wear. You must choose whether to eat breakfast, and If so, what and how much. Before leaving the house, you must decide how you will say good-bye to your family, when and where you will spend time in prayer, and what route you will take to work. Once there, you will make countless decisions related to your job. Then you will need to decide whether you will skip lunch or go out for something to eat.

All Decisions Are Important

Obviously, some decisions are more important than others. Deciding to eat two slices of toast with jelly for breakfast would not have the same significance as choosing to go to bed early because you are performing surgery the next day. Still, even the most trivial decisions you make hold the potential for good or bad consequences.

For instance, eating two slices of toast with jelly in the morning would seem inconsequential unless you are diabetic. What shoes to wear to work doesn't seem like a big decision unless there is ice outside and the shoes have no traction. Poor choices often produce unpleasant consequences, and in the same way, making wise decisions can bring you significant rewards.

Reason #4: You need wisdom to counter the devil's tactics.

You have a real adversary. His name is Satan. He was once the highest of all the angels surrounding God's throne. But when he began to think too highly of himself, he and those angels who participated in his rebellion were cast out of heaven. Now he and his fallen angels roam the earth. Their mission is to derail God's plan for your life. Satan and his minions are invisible, ruthless, and evil. First Peter 5:8 says this: "Be sober, be vigilant; because your adversary the devil walks about like a roaring lion, seeking whom he may devour."

Satan is on your trail all right. Though he would like to deceive you into thinking he's not, Ephesians 6:12 says: "We do not wrestle against flesh and blood, but against principalities, against powers, against the rulers of the darkness of this age, against spiritual hosts of wickedness in the heavenly places."

Standing alone, we are no match for Satan, but when we stand in the strength and power of our Savior Jesus Christ, the evil deceiver cannot touch us. Read Philippians 2:5–11:

Let this mind be in you which was also in Christ Jesus, who, being in the form of God, did not consider it to robbery to be equal with God, but made Himself of no reputation, taking the form of a bondservant, and coming in the likeness of men. And being found in appearance as a man, He humbled Himself and became obedient to the point of death, even the death of the cross. Therefore God also has highly exalted Him and given Him the name which is above every name, that at the name of

Jesus every knee should bow, of those in heaven, and of those on earth, and of those under the earth, and that every tongue should confess that Jesus Christ is Lord, to the glory of God the Father.

Jesus stripped Satan of his authority and power when He rose from the dead and triumphed over the curse of sin. He has also supplied us with weapons to fight against our adversary and accuser. They are the powerful name of Jesus, the Bible—God's living Word—and the blood of the Lamb, which Jesus shed on the cross.

Though Satan no longer has real power over us, there is no doubt that he will do his best to trip us up and pull us away from God's plan and purpose for our lives. He will use any crack in the door or chink in our armor to get in and wreak havoc in our lives. First Peter 5:8 says to be sober and vigilant. That means to be proactive and make good decisions to counter his devices, "Lest Satan should take advantage of us; for we are not ignorant of his devices" (2 Corinthians 2:11).

God wants us to be aware of Satan's tactics. Professional sports teams spend a lot of time studying their opponents' plays and habits. This information helps them to anticipate what will happen on the field of play. We are to do the same with Satan. Studying the Word of God enables us to understand our opponent and his tactics. The more time we spend studying God's Word, the more predictable the devil becomes. Good preparation leads to good decision making and ultimately victory over our adversary.

Reason #5: Wisdom requires less effort and makes finishing your course enjoyable.

During my days in the military, I often heard the saying, "Work smarter; not harder." Working harder doesn't always translate into productivity. That's why many people who sincerely want to achieve great things for God become frustrated. They assume they are expected to burn the candle at both ends to achieve their goals or please God. Nothing could be further from the truth! Please do not misunderstand me. I believe in working hard, but I believe God's instruction to "work *wiser* and not harder" is far better. Working wisely, or efficiently, always translates into productivity. Solomon put it this way: "If the ax is dull, and one does not sharpen the edge, then he must use more strength; but wisdom brings success" (Ecclesiastes 10:10).

Picture yourself as the person in the previous illustration. Do you want to have a sharp ax or a dull ax in your hand? With a sharp ax you may be able to cut down twenty trees in one day. With a dull ax you may only cut down one. Imagine working so hard with so little to show for it! Think of it this way: A sharp ax represents wisdom. You can have great faith, but if your ax is dull you are only going to cut down one tree instead of twenty. Operating in wisdom has great rewards and requires less effort. "When a man's ways please the LORD, He makes even his enemies to be at peace with him" (Proverbs 16:7). Speaking of wisdom, Solomon said: "Her ways are ways of pleasantness, and all her paths are peace" (Proverbs 3:17).

Hosea 4:6 says: "My people are destroyed for lack of knowledge." Knowledge is one of the two components of wisdom. It encompasses not only revelation knowledge of God and His Word but also conventional knowledge. Therefore, the first part of Hosea 4:6 could also be understood to say, "My people are destroyed for lack of wisdom." People often go through unnecessary hardship because they don't possess the wisdom they need to make good decisions.

Remember: wisdom is not only making *good* decisions but also eliminating *bad* ones.

This might sound pretty silly at first, but think of it this way: You can choose to make a good decision or you can choose not to make a bad one. Say you make a decision to stay away from fatty foods because your latest physical revealed a high cholesterol level. That's a good decision. A few days later, you find yourself with a bag of potato chips in your hand. You have made a bad decision. Fortunately, though, you aren't locked into your bad decision. You can eliminate it by crushing the bag of chips and throwing it in the trash. Good decisions have the potential to lift you up, but bad decisions can pull you down. Eliminate them and make the good decision to avoid those bad decisions in the future.

Making all these good and bad decisions could leave you feeling like life is one big struggle. But the Bible tells us that there is rest in doing the right thing, choosing the good path, acting wisely. Hebrews 4:9–11 says: "There remains therefore a rest for the people of God. For he who has entered His rest has himself also ceased from his works as God did from His. Let us therefore be diligent to enter that rest, lest anyone fall according to the same example of disobedience."

Notice that the last word in this passage of scripture is *disobedience*. Why do people disobey God? They do so out of a lack of faith and a lack of wisdom. Jesus Himself talked about entering into His rest in the midst of life's challenges. "Take My yoke upon you and learn from Me, for I am gentle and lowly in heart, and you will find rest for your souls. For My yoke is easy and My burden is light" (Matthew 11:29–30).

The key words I want to emphasize to you from this passage are *learn from Me*. Here the Lord Jesus is inviting us to acquire His wisdom that we may enjoy rest in the midst of our daily lives. Wisdom requires less effort and makes finishing your course enjoyable.

Have you ever been on an airplane that was flying smoothly one minute and the next minute encountering turbulence? Do you remember how uncomfortable that was and how difficult it was to focus or get anything else done? The consequences of poor decision making are like the turbulence on that plane ride. The devil wants you to make poor decisions so that you will have turbulence in your life, maybe even crash or live a miserable existence. Wisdom helps eliminate turbulence by enabling you to make good decisions.

DISCUSSION

1. What do you believe to be God's plan for your life?

2. How significant is wisdom in fulfilling God's plan for your life?

3. Why does wisdom work in all circumstances?

4. Why is wisdom essential in countering the devil's tactics?

5. How can wisdom make your life smoother and more enjoyable?

CHAPTER 2

Consider and Understand Your Ways

CONSIDER YOUR WAYS

The book of Haggai tells how God instructed the children of Israel to consider their ways. A group of exiles returned to Jerusalem from Persia in 536 BC and began reconstructing the temple of God by building an altar and laying the foundation. The work came to a standstill; however, when people became more interested in fixing up their own houses than the house of the Lord. For fifteen long years, the temple project went unattended, and then God sent Haggai to bring His people a message of correction and encouragement as we see in Haggai 1:2–11:

> *Thus speaks the LORD of hosts, saying: "This people says, 'The time has not come, the time that the LORD's house should be built.'" Then the word of the LORD came by Haggai the prophet, saying, "Is it time for you yourselves to dwell in your paneled houses, and this temple to lie in ruins?" Now therefore, thus says the LORD of hosts: "Consider your ways! "You have sown much, and bring in little; you eat, but do not have enough; you drink, but you are not filled with drink; you clothe yourselves, but no*

one is warm; and he who earns wages, earns wages to put into a bag with holes." Thus says the LORD of hosts: "Consider your ways! Go up to the mountains and bring wood and build the temple, that I may take pleasure in it and be glorified," says the LORD. "You looked for much, but indeed it came to little; and when you brought it home, I blew it away. Why?" says the LORD of hosts. "Because of My house that is in ruins, while every one of you runs to his own house. Therefore the heavens above you withhold the dew, and the earth withholds its fruit. For I called for a drought on the land and the mountains, on the grain and the new wine and the oil, on whatever the ground brings forth, on men and livestock, and on all the labor of your hands."

The people heard the word of the Lord to *consider their ways.* The children of Israel had already spent seventy years in exile because of sin against God. They realized that they had selfishly neglected the construction of God's house. The Lord and His house were not being honored and thus people were missing out on God's blessing and risking further judgment. Only after the people considered their ways did they decide to obey the voice of the Lord. "Zerubbabel the son of Shealtiel, and Joshua the son of Jehozadak, the high priest, with all the remnant of the people, obeyed the voice of the LORD their God, and the words of Haggai the prophet, as the LORD their God had sent him; and the people feared the presence of the LORD" (Haggai 1:12).

Once the people of Israel had responded to Haggai's message and considered their ways and changed their hearts, the Lord sent them a word of encouragement. "Haggai, the LORD's messenger, spoke the Lord's message to the people, saying, 'I am with you, says the Lord'" (Haggai 1:13).

During my years in the military, our family changed local churches with each new duty station. The new local church would often be in the middle of a construction project. During these building projects I would remember God telling the children of Israel in Haggai to consider their ways. I often would stop to consider if I was putting my house and personal comfort before God's house and the honor that was His due. My wife and I have always believed in giving generously to the construction of God's house. My prayer has been, "Lord, if I build Your house and honor You then I know You will build my house and honor me." When I pray that way I am referring not only to our house, but also our family. God has been faithful over the years to provide a good home for us and take care of our family. If you honor God, He will honor you. It is important to consider your ways.

UNDERSTAND YOUR WAYS

There is a difference between considering and understanding. Consider means to think over or ponder. Understanding means to comprehend. Both are important aspects of good decision making. You make decisions all the time. How much time do you spend evaluating your decisions to determine if they're good ones? What criteria do you use to help decide if you are making a right choice? It is necessary that you do this because all decisions are important. Proverbs 14:8 says: "The wisdom of the prudent is to understand his way, but the folly of fools is deceit."

There is no such thing as a small decision, just as there is no such thing as a small surgery. I have been practicing obstetrics and gynecology since 1992. During that time I have performed thousands of surgeries and worked with surgeons who have many years of experience. Every surgery, no matter how small, has the potential for an unexpected complication. Complications are rare, but they do happen. For example, a patient can develop a complication due to anesthesia, bleeding, infection, or drug reaction, just to name a few. You can do everything right and still have a complication. Things happen. This is why we take what we do in the OR so seriously. We understand things can deteriorate rapidly. During an operation, the OR team is constantly evaluating what they are doing to make sure the patient has the best chance of a good outcome.

A surgical procedure consists of a number of decisions that when put together produce a desired result. Your daily life should be no different. It is important to evaluate the decisions in your life if you want a good outcome. Keep in mind that in life, like surgery, things happen even when you haven't done anything wrong. You still have to keep moving forward and not allow one complication to stop you from fulfilling your destiny. You need to focus on the things you can control and trust God

for the rest. Consider and understand your ways so that you do
not suffer loss. Proverbs 2:10–11 says: "When wisdom enters
your heart, and knowledge is pleasant to your soul, discretion
will preserve you; understanding will keep you."

A prudent man foresees evil and hides himself,
but the simple pass on and are
punished.—Proverbs 22:3

DISCUSSION

1. Do you regularly stop to consider your ways?

2. What kind of questions do you ask yourself when you
   consider your ways?

3. What is the difference between considering and
   understanding?

4. How do you evaluate your decisions? Explain.

5. Why is it important to evaluate your decisions?

CHAPTER 3

Three Kinds of Decisions

The LORD is my shepherd; I shall not want.
He makes me to lie down in green pastures;
He leads me beside the still waters.
He restores my soul;
He leads me in the paths of righteousness for His
name's sake.—Psalm 23:1–3

The twenty-third psalm beautifully illustrates that we are to cooperate with God in the paths we take in life through our decisions. All decisions are important, but not all decisions are alike. It is important to understand what type of decision you are making at any given time. There are three general types of decisions, with some overlap between them. The requirements and consequences of each type of decision vary. The three types are as follows:

1. Daily living decisions

2. Ethical decisions

3. Goal-oriented decisions

DAILY LIVING DECISIONS

Daily living decisions are just that—decisions you make in the course of your everyday life. They are the most common and, seemingly, the most trivial. Sometimes you make these decisions without a second thought because they come one right after another. They are almost second nature. Examples include getting ready in the morning, driving to work, performing your job, eating your lunch, buying the groceries, doing chores at home, or exercising.

Making these decisions wisely can be a source of physical, emotional, and financial prosperity. They can also bring great blessing, sometimes in the form of divine appointments. "Get wisdom!

Get understanding! Do not forget, nor turn away from the words of my mouth. Do not forsake her, and she will preserve you; love her, and she will keep you" (Proverbs 4:5–6).

Blessings through Daily Living Decisions:

- Rebekah was drawing water from the well in her hometown when she met the envoy of her future husband, Isaac. (See Genesis 24:40–48.)

- Joseph, though innocent, was serving in prison when he was called by Pharaoh to interpret his dreams, and then made second-in-command over Egypt. (See Genesis 41:14–45.)

- Moses was tending the flock of his father-in-law, Jethro, when he encountered God at the burning bush. (See Exodus 3:1–3.)

- Ruth the Moabitess, mentioned in the genealogy of Jesus, was gleaning leftover heads of grain from the fields when she met a wealthy businessman named Boaz. (See Ruth 2:1–3.)

- David was tending his father's sheep when Samuel anointed him king of Israel, and the Spirit of God came upon him from that day forward. (See 1 Samuel 16:1–13.)

- Peter and Andrew were fishing in the Sea of Galilee when they met Jesus, who said to them, "Follow Me, and I will make you fishers of men." (See Matthew 4:18–19.)

What do these people have in common? Notice how every-one I mentioned was busy working and being productive. The Bible says God blesses those who work hard, live with integrity, and are faithful. Consider these two scriptures from the book of Proverbs: "He who has a slack hand becomes poor, but the hand of the diligent makes rich" (Proverbs 10:4), and "The righteous man walks in his integrity; his children are blessed after him" (Proverbs 20:7).

This principle is confirmed in the New Testament: "Well done, good and faithful servant; you were faithful over a few things, I will make you ruler over many things. Enter into the joy of your Lord" (Matthew 25:21).

Solomon put it this way: "Whoever keeps the fig tree will eat its fruit; so he who waits on his master will be honored" (Proverbs 27:18).

Growing in Character Day by Day

Divine appointments are wonderful and exciting, but it is in our day-to-day lives that God molds our character. If we do things God's way, our entire lives should be spent growing in knowledge and character. I am still growing as a physician, husband, parent, and Christian. I am constantly evaluating my walk. God has more for us as we grow in every area of our lives. Let's look at some examples.

- Rebekah grew up in her house learning to do menial chores *before* she became Abraham's daughter-in-law.

- Joseph was in prison for almost thirteen years *before* Pharaoh gave him his signet ring.

- Moses was in exile for forty years *before* God called him to deliver the children of Israel out of Egypt.

- Ruth left everything behind in Moab to follow Naomi *before* she lived the greatest love story in the Old Testament.

- David was persecuted for years by Saul *before* he became king of Judah at age thirty-three, and over all Israel seven years later.

- Peter and Andrew were fishermen all their lives *before* Jesus called them into full-time ministry.

God uses your life experiences to shape your character *before* He sends you out to undertake His great plan for you. Romans 8:28 says: "We know that all things work together for good to those who love God, to those who are the called according to His purpose."

There are two principles of daily living decisions that are important for you to know:

One poor daily living decision can be devastating physically, emotionally, and financially.

Daily living decisions will often force you into an ethical decision.

ONE POOR DAILY LIVING DECISION CAN BE DEVASTATING PHYSICALLY, EMOTIONALLY, AND FINANCIALLY.

When I mention to someone that I'm writing a book on decision making, I inevitably get one of two responses. One response goes something like this: "A book on decision making is really needed. I'll be sure to get a copy when it comes out." The second response usually involves someone telling me how "a poor decision cost them dearly." I got the second type of response when I was in Texas recently, visiting friends. They shared the following about a friend in their church:

> *The area had recently experienced heavy rain and the authorities warned local residents to avoid flooded roadways. Their friend had to take a road that crossed a river in order to reach her destination. The river was partially out of its banks and water covered a portion of the road, but she was in a hurry. She wrestled with the need to get to her destination and the uneasy feeling that gripped her when she looked at the waters moving across the road. For a moment she considered turning back, but then made the decision to cross a flooded road and began driving into the water. She quickly realized her mistake when the waters rushed up around the car and the engine stalled. The authorities had to come to her rescue. In one brief moment, this dear lady lost her car and almost lost her life.*

As an obstetrician, I have the opportunity to help patients during their pregnancies and the privilege of delivering their children. For me there is nothing more rewarding in medicine than bringing a new life into the world. Sometimes, however, patients endanger themselves and their babies by making poor choices like missing appointments, not taking prescribed medications, illegal drug use, and remaining in abusive relationships, just to name a few.

The Bible is filled with stories about people who made poor decisions that cost them dearly. Hezekiah is a good example.

Hezekiah

The story of the Babylonian envoys to King Hezekiah is told in 2 Kings 20:12–19 and Isaiah 39:1–8. When the son of the king of Babylon heard that King Hezekiah was sick, he sent envoys, letters, and a present as a "get well" gesture. Unfortunately, during the envoys' visit, Hezekiah foolishly showed the Babylonians the entire wealth of the kingdom. The Bible says in Isaiah 39:2, "There was nothing in his house or in all his dominion that Hezekiah did not show them." When Isaiah the prophet discovered what Hezekiah had done, he said to the king in Isaiah 39:5–7:

> *Hear the word of the LORD of hosts: "Behold, the days are coming when all that is in your house, and what your fathers have accumulated until this day, shall be carried to Babylon; nothing shall be left,' says the Lord. 'And they shall take away some of your sons who will descend from you, whom you will beget; and they shall be eunuchs in the palace of the king of Babylon."*

I often wonder if Hezekiah's foolishness precipitated the Babylonian captivity that was to come.

DAILY LIVING DECISIONS OFTEN FORCE YOU INTO
AN ETHICAL DECISION.

This point is better explained by examining the story of David and Bathsheba.

David's adultery with Bathsheba, and the devastation that followed, started with a simple decision by David to go for a walk on the roof of his house one evening. "It happened one evening that David arose from his bed and walked on the roof of the king's house. And from the roof he saw a woman bathing, and the woman was very beautiful to behold" (2 Samuel 11:2).

It seems clear that David had no intention of sinning against the Lord as he walked on his roof that night. When he saw Bathsheba bathing, however, things changed. A simple daily living decision now forced him into an ethical decision. David sent and inquired about the woman. And someone said, "Is this not Bathsheba, the daughter of Eliam, the wife of Uriah the Hittite?" (2 Samuel 11:3).

Perhaps if David had paused to consider and understand his ways, the story would have played out differently. But instead he made a poor ethical decision—to find out more about the woman he had seen. That decision, as is often the case, led to yet another poor ethical decision. "David sent messengers, and took her; and she came to him, and he lay with her, for she was cleansed from her impurity; and she returned to her house. And the woman conceived; so she sent and told David, and said, 'I am with child'" (2 Samuel 11:4–5).

Bathsheba's pregnancy through adultery now required David to make yet another series of ethical decisions in which he failed miserably. The rest of 2 Samuel 11 tells the story of David's iniquity. David brought Uriah, Bathsheba's husband, and one of his mighty men back from the battlefield. He tried on two occasions to send Uriah home with the idea that he would have an opportunity to be with his wife and thus cloak David's sin through deception. But Uriah honorably refused to return home to his wife while his men were out on the battlefield undergoing hardship. David then sent Uriah back to the battlefield with a letter containing instructions for his death to be arranged during combat. David's orders were carried out and Uriah died. This portion of the story ends this way: "When her mourning was over, David sent and brought her to his house, and she became his wife and bore him a son. But the thing that David had done displeased the LORD" (2 Samuel 11:27).

The tragic events in the lives of David, Bathsheba, and Uriah started with a simple daily living decision. David's decision to go for a walk on his roof one night forced him into an ethical decision. Elements of this scenario enter our everyday lives through television, movies, the Internet, and other daily living activities. Simple choices lead to ethical choices when seductive images and perverse behaviors are played out before our eyes. Satan is very adept at using these opportunities to tempt us to sin, just as he did with Jesus. Read Luke 4:13: "When the devil had ended every temptation, he departed from Him until an opportune time."

A daily living decision like watching television or a movie can force you, like David, into an ethical decision. At that point, you have an opportunity to make a good ethical decision.

Sexual sin is one of the primary ways in which Satan keeps men and women in bondage. Paul warns the church about this in Galatians 5:19–21, where he talks about the lusts of the flesh. The first four of the seventeen lusts of the flesh listed in that passage of scripture deal with sexual sin. They are adultery, fornication, uncleanness, and lewdness.

David knew God. He was anointed with the Holy Spirit. He wrote many of the Psalms. He had wealth, fame, and power, and it wasn't enough to stop him from doing what he did. He lacked the wisdom to make a good ethical decision on this occasion. All it takes is one poor decision to bring someone down. God can forgive and restore when there is true repentance, like He did with David, but there is also a price to pay. David could have avoided this pitfall, and consequences, if only he had utilized the right decision-making process.

What about Joseph?

Joseph, on the other hand, made a good decision when he refused the sexual advances of Potiphar's wife. She pressed false charges against Joseph and he spent almost thirteen years in prison. The day came, however, when God promoted Joseph to a position second only to Pharaoh over all of Egypt. Why? When Joseph's daily living decision forced him into an ethical decision, he chose wisely. You can read all about Joseph and his encounter with Potiphar's wife in Genesis 39:7–23.

You and I transition from daily living decisions to ethical decisions all the time. We have a choice to compromise like David, or do what is right, like Joseph. We have to decide between what feels good and what is right. David decided to do what feels good. Joseph decided to do what is right. Operating in wisdom is not based on feelings, but rather conviction. There will sometimes be a price to pay for honoring your conviction. Joseph spent thirteen years in prison as a result of his decision to do the right thing. The day came, however, when God promoted him to second in Egypt *because* of his convictions.

So what constitutes an ethical decision?

Ethical Decisions

Ethical decisions are based on the standard of God's Word, the Bible. Matthew 4:4 tells us this: "He answered and said, 'It is written, "Man shall not live by bread alone, but by every word that proceeds from the mouth of God."'" The Psalmist

agrees: "Your word I have hidden in my heart, that I might not sin against You" (Psalm 119:11).

In Exodus 20 God gave us the Ten Commandments as a foundation for our conduct. The basis or motivation for that conduct is love. Jesus put it this way in Matthew 22:35–40:

> *One of them, a lawyer, asked Him a question, testing Him, and saying, "Teacher, which is the greatest commandment in the law?" Jesus said to him, "'You shall love the LORD your God with all your heart, with all your soul, and with all your mind.' This is the first and great commandment. And the second is like it: 'You shall love your neighbor as yourself.' On these two commandments hang all the Law and the Prophets."*

Obeying God's Word brings about blessing, while disobeying God's Word brings about destruction. Proverbs 13:13 says, "He who despises the word will be destroyed, but he who fears the commandment will be rewarded."

It's important to know that not every transition from a daily living decision to an ethical decision is as dramatic as it was in the stories of David and Joseph. Even those transitions that seem minor should be regarded with great wisdom. Consider this story about an employee named Bill.

It is now the end of the day at the corporate office where Bill works. He is preparing to pick up his satchel and go home. He sees a pen and notepad on his desk that belongs to his employer. He is now debating about taking them home for his personal use. Bill makes a poor ethical decision by picking them up and putting them in his satchel. Bill has just made the decision to steal. He has just opened the door for Satan to begin to wreak havoc in his life. The integrity of Bill's decision-making armor has been compromised and exposed for the enemy to strike.

The Word of God is our standard. The more Satan can convince you to compromise, the more control he will have over you and the more chaos he can cause in your life. The good news is that if you have accepted Jesus Christ as your Savior and genuinely repent of sin, God is willing and able to forgive you. In 1 John 1:9 we read: "If we confess our sins, He is faithful and just to forgive us our sins and to cleanse us from all unrighteousness."

Pause for a moment and ask yourself if you have allowed these little foxes of compromise and disobedience to God's Word to place you in danger. We are to catch and get rid of these little foxes lest they cut off God's fruitfulness in our lives. "Catch us the foxes, the little foxes that spoil the vines, for our vines have tender grapes" (Song of Solomon 2:15).

Goal-Oriented Decisions

The third and last category of decisions is goal-oriented decisions. These are decisions that are directed toward a well-defined goal or objective. The goal may be personal or God-given. For example, a personal goal might be to improve your communication skills or change your eating habits. A God-given goal might be to complete a project God has given you. Wisdom is required in order to achieve personal and God-given goals.  "A wise man scales the city of the mighty, and brings down the trusted stronghold" (Proverbs 21:22). Let's look closely at God-given goals.

THE GREATER THE GOAL, THE GREATER
THE WISDOM OR DECISION MAKING THAT IS
REQUIRED TO ACHIEVE THE GOAL.

God-given goals are directly from God to an individual. These goals are very specific. They are God's way of saying, *"This is the mission and I have chosen you to carry it out."* Noah's ark is an example. Here are some other Bible examples:

1. Abraham moving from Ur of the Chaldeans to Canaan

2. Joseph's administration in Egypt during the years of plenty and famine

3. Moses leading the children of Israel out of Egyptian bondage

4. Moses building the tabernacle in the wilderness

5. Joshua leading Israel to conquest and possession of the promised land

6. Deborah and Barak liberating Israel from Canaanite oppression

7. Gideon's defeat of the Midianites

8. Solomon building the temple of the Lord

9. Elijah's Mount Carmel victory over the prophets of Baal

10. Jonah being sent to preach at Nineveh

Faith Projects

Sometimes a God-given goal can start off as a faith project. A person sees a great need that grieves their heart. They present the situation to the Lord in prayer. By faith that person starts doing what they can to meet the need, trusting God will be with them. God blesses their work and helps see it to completion.

Nehemiah rebuilding the walls of Jerusalem is a good example of this type of faith project. The book of Nehemiah in the Bible tells his story. Nehemiah, a Hebrew, was the cupbearer for the king of Persia. He learned that among the Judean survivors of the Babylonian captivity there was great distress and reproach. The walls of Jerusalem had been broken down and the gates had been burned. The Bible says that Nehemiah wept, fasted, and prayed for many days before the Lord about this plight. God granted Nehemiah favor with the king, who helped him with the authority and supplies to not only rebuild the walls of Jerusalem, but lead a political and spiritual restoration for his people.

For me, writing this book has been this kind of faith project. I saw a great epidemic of deception and poor decision making ruining people's lives. I took this to the Lord in fervent prayer. Over a period of years of study, the Lord has given me, and continues to give me, insights into the decision-making process. These insights are greatly impacting people in a positive way. *The Art of Decision* is my Nehemiah's wall.

Perhaps you are working on a faith project or have one in your dreams. You have seen a great need and your heart's cry is to meet that need. You have taken this issue to the Lord in prayer, and you are taking steps of faith to do something about it. Do not get discouraged. Do what you can when you can, and God will do what no man can. God parted the Red Sea for Moses. He brought down the walls of Jericho for Joshua. He will do the same for you. Just keep moving forward one day at a time and do what God requires. He will do the rest.

The Art of Decision will take you step by step through the process of achieving your faith projects. I believe the principles in this book will help you greatly. I can't wait for you to read the rest of the book. I believe it will be a blessing to you.

The Cross: the Greatest Faith Project Ever

God's plan of redemption for mankind through the death, burial, and resurrection of Jesus Christ is the greatest faith project ever. Jesus saw a need due to the spiritual death of mankind brought on by Adam's sin. "Just as through one man sin entered the world, and death through sin, and thus death spread to all men, because all sinned" (Romans 5:12).

Jesus stepped out in faith believing God would bless His sacrifice. We receive Jesus by faith. He laid down His life for us by faith. We read in Romans 3:25: "Whom God set forth as propitiation by His blood, through faith."

Jesus' act of faith on the cross for us was motivated by unconditional love. "God demonstrates His own love toward us, in that while we were still sinners, Christ died for us" (Romans 5:8).

Jesus' act of unconditional love has made salvation available to all through faith in Him! "God so loved the world that He gave His only begotten Son, that whoever believes in Him should not perish but have everlasting life" (John 3:16).

THE GREATER THE GOAL,
THE GREATER THE WISDOM THAT IS REQUIRED,

Jesus' crucifixion was not only His greatest act of faith and love, but also His greatest act of wisdom. Consider these two New Testament scriptures: 1 Corinthians 1:22–24 says: "Jews request a sign, and Greeks seek after wisdom; but we preach Christ crucified, to the Jews a stumbling block and to the Greeks foolishness, but to those who are called, both Jews and Greeks, Christ the power of God and the wisdom of God." We read in Colossians 2:2–3: "To the knowledge of the mystery of God, both of the Father and of Christ, in whom are hidden all the treasures of wisdom and knowledge."

Goal-oriented decisions, whether God-given or faith projects, are unique for a couple of reasons. Goal-oriented decisions differ from daily living and ethical decisions in that

1. They require more of a certain type of knowledge;

2. There is a well-defined objective.

Faith and Wisdom Work Together

I have shared with you how the Lord
showed me that faith and wisdom work
together like gears.

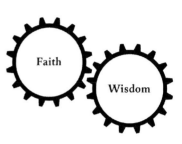

*Faith that is not tempered by wisdom
is like a loose cannon or an arrow without
feathers. Wisdom gives faith direction.*

Let me give you some other concepts about faith and wisdom
working together. I previously shared the following with you:

Faith	Wisdom
Sees	*Enables*
Answers the *what* to believe	Answers the *how* to obtain what you believe

Wisdom and faith are connected to each other because they
share a common denominator. That common denominator is
knowledge. Revelation knowledge of God's Word is the link
between faith and wisdom.

In chapter one I began telling you about the connection
between faith and wisdom. I shared with you that faith comes
by revelation knowledge of God's Word. "Faith comes by hearing, and hearing by the word of God" (Romans 10:17).

Wisdom also comes by revelation knowledge of God's Word.
"That the God of our Lord Jesus Christ, the Father of glory, may
give to you the spirit of wisdom and revelation in the knowledge
of Him" (Ephesians 1:17).

What distinguishes godly faith from godly wisdom is that
godly wisdom encompasses more than revelation knowledge of

God's Word. There are different categories of knowledge. There are also simple, but specific, rules regarding how that knowledge works. I call these the twelve rules of knowledge. I explain these rules in detail in chapter six. The principal things I want you to remember are the following:

1. Faith and wisdom come from God.

2. Faith and wisdom work together harmoniously.

3. Faith and wisdom are both essential for your success.

There is another way to look at the relationship between faith and wisdom.

Faith + Wisdom = Victory

Faith sees the victory.

Wisdom enables you to obtain the victory.

Faith + Wisdom = Vision Accomplished

Faith sees the vision. Wisdom enables you to fulfill the vision.

Mountain Climbing Faith and Wisdom

Picture yourself standing at the foot of a mountain you are about to climb. By faith you look up and see yourself standing on the peak. You need faith to climb that mountain, don't you? Faith alone, however, will not get you to the top. You can stay at the foot of that mountain for twenty years and by faith believe that you will reach the top and go nowhere. You see people pass by on their way up the mountain, but you are still at the bottom. You look up and still see yourself standing at the peak but haven't moved an inch toward your goal. You are now twenty years older and nothing has changed. Why, you ask? The reason for this is that in order to reach the top you have to have *corresponding actions*. Corresponding actions require good *decisions*. Good decisions require *wisdom*. This is where wisdom kicks in with your faith. It's that simple.

My purpose in this book is to show you *how* to combine your faith with God's wisdom, or principles of decision making, as He has shown me. I believe these principles will serve like climbing tools and a navigation map, *enabling* you to reach your mountaintop while *avoiding* treacherous pitfalls along the way. My goal is to make you a master decision-making mountain climber. These principles will work regardless of whether you are making daily, ethical, or goal-oriented decisions.

Following these principles has many benefits for your life. First, you will be able to accomplish things you never thought you could do. Second, you will require less time and effort in achieving the God-given dreams and goals you have in your heart. Third, and for me most importantly, you will experience the joy of a loving God partnering with you through each of the seven steps on the way to your mountaintop. Living by *these principles* is a supernatural adventure with God Himself!

DISCUSSION

1. What are the three categories of decisions?

2. True or false: One poor daily living decision can be devastating physically, emotionally, and financially.

3. True or false: Daily living decisions will often force you into an ethical decision.

4. Give examples of how one poor daily living decision can be devastating physically, emotionally, and economically.

5. Give examples of how daily living decisions will often force you into ethical decisions.

6. What is the standard for ethical decisions?

7. True and false: Poor ethical decisions, no matter how seemingly trivial, are still sin.

8. What is the difference between a God-given goal and a faith project?

9. What is your God-given goal or faith project?

10. How do faith and wisdom work together like gears in achieving your goals and fulfilling your God-given dreams?

CHAPTER 4

The Wisest Man Who Ever Lived

God declared Solomon to be the wisest man who ever lived. (See 1 Kings 4:29–34.) The story of his life is found in the first eleven chapters of 1 Kings and the first nine chapters of 2 Chronicles. Nineteen chapters tell of his great accomplishments, and one chapter tells of his failures and decline. These scriptures reveal some of the characteristics that made Solomon a great man. Jesus mentions Solomon four times in the Gospels. The first two are Matthew 6:28–29 and Luke 12:27: "Why do you worry about clothing? Consider the lilies of the field, how they grow: they neither toil nor spin; and yet I say to you that even Solomon in all his glory was not arrayed like one of these." The second two are in Matthew 12:42 and Luke 11:31: "The queen of the South will rise up in the judgment with this generation and condemn it, for she came from the ends of the earth to hear the wisdom of Solomon; and indeed a greater than Solomon is here."

Jesus confirmed the queen of the South, or queen of Sheba, visited Solomon. She came from the ends of the earth to hear his wisdom. Jesus was teaching a principle about growing in wisdom: in order to grow in wisdom you have to invest of your time, energy, and resources.

The five "wisdom books" in the Bible are Job, Psalms, Proverbs, Ecclesiastes, and Song of Solomon. The author of Job is uncertain, but some consider Solomon a possibility. He is credited with writing Psalm 72 and Psalm 127. In addition to all but two chapters in Proverbs, Solomon is also the author of Ecclesiastes and Song of Solomon. The Bible also tells us in 1 Kings 4:32: "He spoke three thousand proverbs, and his songs were one thousand and five." A great deal can be learned by summarizing the highs and lows of Solomon's life.

CHARACTERISTICS OF SOLOMON'S LIFE

1. Solomon acquired his wisdom through humility.

Humility is a primary ingredient in successful leadership. Proverbs 3:34 says: "Surely He scorns the scornful, but gives grace to the humble." Then in James 4:10 we read: "Humble yourselves in the sight of the Lord, and He will lift you up."

At the beginning of his reign, Solomon went to Gibeon to offer one thousand burnt offerings to the Lord. The young ruler was seeking God to help him lead the nation of Israel. He was following in the footsteps of his father, King David, and though he would not admit it publicly, he felt overwhelmed by the great responsibility. Solomon was investing of his *time*, *energy*, and *resources* to grow in wisdom. After his monumental sacrifice, the Lord appeared to Solomon in a dream saying, "Ask! What shall I give you?" Solomon replies to the Lord's offer with humility, describing himself as follows: "I am a little child; I do not know how to go out or come in" (1 Kings 3:7).

Here Solomon applies another principle of wisdom: In order to grow in wisdom, you have to operate in humility. "When pride comes, then comes shame; but with the humble is wisdom" (Proverbs 11:2).

Solomon is operating in humility by acknowledging his dependence on God. Solomon then makes his petition to the Lord. He admits to God that he does not know *how* to lead the people. He asks for an understanding heart and the *ability* to discern between good and evil. Then Solomon asks the Lord for wisdom. Remember that wisdom *enables* and answers the *how* question. Solomon was asking the Lord to *enable* him in *how* to achieve his God-given purpose, which was to lead God's people. His motive for requesting wisdom was to help others.

The primary purpose of wisdom is to help others.

The desire to help others should also be the primary reason for us to grow in wisdom. The Bible says that Solomon's speech pleased the Lord, who answered in this way: "Behold, I have done according to your words; see, I have given you a wise and understanding heart, so that there has not been anyone like you before you, nor shall any like you arise after you" (1 Kings 3:12).

What a promise! Solomon became the wisest man who has ever lived or will ever live! Think about that for a moment. God instantly gave Solomon the greatest *ability* to make wise decisions of any person ever. The Lord downloaded the biblical decision-making process into Solomon's mind.

God also granted Solomon riches and honor. The Lord promised him a long life if he would walk in His ways. These are three of the benefits of wisdom: riches, honor, and a prolonged life. In summary, Solomon acquired God's wisdom, and its benefits, by approaching the Lord with humility.

2. Solomon's wisdom became immediately evident.

Solomon's wisdom was soon put to the test. He had to decide between two women which one was the rightful mother of a newborn infant. Both women claimed to be the mother. One was obviously lying. Solomon's solution was to take a sword and cut the child in two, giving half to each mother. One woman agreed with the plan to split the child between them, while the other begged him to spare the child and give it to the other woman. Solomon rightly deduced that the compassionate woman was the child's mother.

God's wisdom in Solomon became immediately evident to the nation, giving them confidence in his leadership. "All Israel heard of the judgment which the king had rendered; and they feared the king, for they saw that the wisdom of God was in him to administer justice" (1 Kings 3:28).

When you have wisdom, people will show confidence in you. The ability to lead people wisely will determine the extent of your influence. "In a multitude of people is a king's honor, but in the lack of people is the downfall of a prince" (Proverbs 14:28).

The judgment of Solomon in the case of the two women and the infant brought honor to Solomon and glory to God.

Remember the three benefits of wisdom: riches, honor, and prolonged life. What God did for Solomon He will also do for you. Romans 2:11 confirms this: "There is no partiality with God." The same principle is repeated in Galatians 2:6: "God shows personal favoritism to no man."

3. Solomon had a kingdom that was well organized, prosperous, peaceful, and safe, and attracted people from all over the world.

First Kings 4 gives us a description of Solomon's organized kingdom. It describes Israel's national order of priests, scribes, recorder, military commander, the king's household, labor force, and governors, and tells us that the land enjoyed great prosperity under Solomon's leadership. We read: "Judah and Israel were as numerous as the sand by the sea in multitude, eating and drinking and rejoicing. So Solomon reigned over all kingdoms from the River to the land of the Philistines, as far as the border of Egypt. They brought tribute and served Solomon all the days of his life" (1 Kings 4:20–21).

Israel was also peaceful and safe during Solomon's reign. "He had peace on every side all around him. And Judah and Israel dwelt safely, each man under his vine and his fig tree, from Dan as far as Beersheba, all the days of Solomon" (1 Kings 4:24–25).

From "Dan to Beersheba" means from the northernmost to the southernmost parts of the kingdom. In other words, the entire nation enjoyed peace and safety. All the kings of the earth who heard of Solomon sent representatives to him. These rulers wanted to hear the wisdom of King David's son as expressed in 1 Kings 4:34: "Men of all nations, from all the kings of the earth who had heard of his wisdom, came to hear the wisdom of Solomon."

Think of it. Solomon was a mentor to all the kings of the earth. Those kings realized the value of wisdom in effectively governing their own people. They were willing to invest *time, energy,* and *resources* to acquire wisdom from Solomon. In Matthew 12:42 and Luke 11:31, Jesus Himself mentions the value of gaining wisdom. "The queen of the South will rise up in the judgment with the men of this generation and condemn them, for she came from the ends of the earth to hear the wisdom of Solomon; and indeed a greater than Solomon is here" (Luke 11:31).

Investing in wisdom should be a lifestyle, just like prayer and studying God's Word. How are you going to achieve your dreams and God's plan for your life apart from gaining greater wisdom? Wisdom, unlike monetary riches, never loses its value once it is obtained. Proverbs 3:13–15 says: "Happy is the man who finds wisdom, and the man who gains understanding; for her proceeds are better than the profits of silver, and her gain than fine gold. She is more precious than rubies, and all the things you may desire cannot compare with her."

The queen of Sheba and the kings of Solomon's day sought out Solomon for his wisdom. They understood that in order to grow in wisdom, they would have to invest their *time, energy,* and *resources,* but the wisdom they received would never lose its value.

Solomon was able to lead his people in an organized, prosperous, and peaceful manner. Wisdom can enable you to do the same.

4. Solomon was graceful and eloquent in speech.

King Solomon was an exceptional communicator in his time. He had the ability to get things accomplished and forge relationships through his words. He sent a letter to King Hiram of Tyre shortly after he assumed the throne of his father David. Hiram had been friends with David. Solomon's intent in writing Hiram was to negotiate for materials and skilled labor needed to build the temple of the Lord.

> *Solomon sent to Hiram, saying: You know how my father David could not build a house for the name of the LORD his God because of the wars which were fought against him on every side, until the LORD put his foes under the soles of his feet. But now the LORD my God has given me rest on every side; there is neither adversary nor evil occurrence. And behold, I propose to build a house for the name of the LORD my God, as the LORD spoke to my father David, saying, "Your son, whom I will set on your throne in your place, he shall build the house for My name." Now therefore, command that they cut down cedars for me from Lebanon; and my servants will be with your servants, and I will pay you wages for your servants according to whatever you say. For you know there is none among us who has skill to cut timber like the Sidonians* (1 Kings 5:2–6; see also 2 Chronicles 2:3–10).

Who can say no to a request like that! Solomon begins his letter with a compliment. In the body of the letter he honors Hiram for

1. His knowledge;

2. His friendship with David;

3. His country's natural resources;

4. His integrity as a businessman;

5. His people's skill;

Notice Hiram's response in 1 Kings 5:7: "Blessed be the LORD this day, for He has given David a wise son over this great people!" Hiram was David's neighbor to the north. Now, after one wisely written letter, he became Solomon's ally. Notice again how Solomon received the honor and God received the glory. Solomon's words had the grace of the Spirit of God to accomplish good things.

We can, and should, communicate with others in this way. Proverbs 22:11 says: "He who loves purity of heart and has grace on his lips, the king will be his friend." Then we read in Colossians 4:6: "Let your speech always be with grace, seasoned with salt, that you may know how you ought to answer each one." Once again this principle is affirmed in Ephesians 4:29: "Let no corrupt word proceed out of your mouth, but what is good for necessary edification, that it may impart grace to the hearers."

Solomon knew how to get things done and build relationships through his graceful and eloquent speech. "The LORD gave Solomon wisdom, as He had promised him; and there was peace between Hiram and Solomon, and the two of them made a treaty together" (1 Kings 5:12).

In Proverbs 18:21 Solomon made a powerful statement

about the power of our words. "Death and life are in the power of the tongue, and those who love it will eat its fruit."

Solomon was a master in the art of communication and diplomacy. This God-given ability is something that you and I can and should develop in our lives. For example, I make it my aim to *connect with people, build them up,* and *make them laugh* in the course of a conversation. Here are some practical examples.

When I show up at my clinic, I greet my clerk with the words "Hello, Super!" I do this because for years I have been calling her my "super clerk." She likes being called that so much that she performs like a super clerk. She takes care of everything I need without my asking.

I make it a habit to shake my patients' hands, look them in the eyes, and smile. In my medical practice, I ask patients about smoking. This is often an uncomfortable question for several reasons. They know they should stop smoking but haven't been able to quit. They also fear they will be chastised for something they know is harmful. I can usually tell if a patient smokes by his or her body language even before I ask the question. Instead, I ask, "Did you know smoking is bad for you?" Such a preposterously obvious question breaks the ice and usually brings a smile. If the person is trying to quit but hasn't fully succeeded, I offer encouragement to keep plugging away. Every time we speak, we have an opportunity to make a new friend or strengthen our relationship with an old friend.

5. Solomon built the temple of the Lord in Jerusalem.

The construction of the temple in Jerusalem is one of Solomon's great accomplishments and a highlight in the history of Israel. "Solomon began to build the house of the LORD at Jerusalem on Mount Moriah, where the LORD had appeared to his father David, at the place that David had prepared on the threshing floor of Ornan the Jebusite" (2 Chronicles 3:1).

Solomon employed 153,600 men to complete the seven-year task. "Solomon selected seventy thousand men to bear burdens, eighty thousand to quarry stone in the mountains, and three thousand six hundred to oversee them" (2 Chronicles 2:2).

In 1 Kings 6:37–38 we read: "In the fourth year the foundation of the house of the LORD was laid, in the month of Ziv. And in the eleventh year, in the month of Bul, which is the eighth month, the house was finished in all its details and according to all its plans. So he was seven years in building it."

The temple site in Jerusalem remains the spiritual center of the Jewish people to this day.

6. Solomon was paid a historic visit by the queen of Sheba.

It is believed that Sheba was located in Ethiopia or the Arabian Peninsula. Jesus said Sheba's queen came from the ends of the earth to hear the wisdom of Solomon. This was no casual visit. It cost her something.

When the queen of Sheba heard of Solomon's fame and wisdom, she decided to go to Jerusalem to test him with hard questions. She made the journey to Jerusalem with a great entourage on camels bearing spices, gold, and precious stones as gifts for Solomon. The gold alone weighed one hundred twenty talents, approximately nine thousand pounds! Imagine how many camels were required to carry her people, provisions, and presents for Solomon. The Bible says that she spoke with Solomon about all that was in her heart. In addition to testing Solomon, I believe the queen of Sheba was seeking his advice. Imagine being a female ruler in a male-dominated world. The queen of Sheba no doubt had her share of enemies. She needed a wise person she could trust to speak into her life. She was applying one of the key principles of wisdom.

In order to grow in wisdom you must invest of your time, energy, and resources.

Many kings of the earth heard of Solomon's great wisdom and sent representatives to hear what he had to say. But only the queen of Sheba went in person and only her visit is recorded in detail. Jesus mentions her visit twice. It is clear that the Lord is trying to convey to us the value of obtaining wisdom. Acquiring wisdom is an investment, not an expense. The queen of Sheba did this in dramatic fashion.

Acquiring wisdom is an investment, not an expense.

Let me stop here for a moment and ask you a question: Do you routinely invest *time, energy,* and *resources* to gain knowledge and grow in wisdom? Doing this should be a way of life for you. The more knowledge you have, the more you will potentially be able to achieve. Wisdom never loses its value.

The Bible says Solomon answered all the questions asked by the visiting foreign queen, and she left in awe of his wisdom and prosperity. She praised the Lord God for making him ruler over Israel. Solomon then presented her with many presents before she left for home. "King Solomon gave the queen of Sheba all she desired, whatever she asked, besides what Solomon had given her according to the royal generosity. So she turned and went to her own country, she and her servants" (1 Kings 10:13).

We can learn a great deal from the story of Solomon and the queen of Sheba.

1. When you bless a wise person, you will receive much in return.

2. Wise people are willing to help those who honor them appropriately.

3. When you bless a wise person, you have made a powerful ally.

By following these simple rules, the queen of Sheba now had a powerful friend and ally named Solomon. Make a habit of blessing and honoring the wise people in your life. They will help take you places you could not go on your own. God has strategically placed them in your life to help you reach your destination. They will be there for you in your greatest moment of need.

Valuable Lessons

Now I am going to review some of Solomon's failures. First Kings 11 tells the story of Solomon's tragic decline. There are some valuable lessons here also.

7. *Solomon loved foreign women who turned his heart away from God.*

God had commanded the children of Israel not to marry people from other nations who worshipped other gods, lest their hearts turn away from following Him. "Nor shall you make marriages with them. You shall not give your daughter to their son, nor take their daughter for your son. For they will turn your sons away from following Me, to serve other gods; so the anger of the LORD will be aroused against you and destroy you suddenly" (Deuteronomy 7:3–4).

Solomon made a strategic mistake at the beginning of his reign. He married Pharaoh's daughter for the sake of creating a political alliance. "Solomon made a treaty with Pharaoh king of Egypt, and married Pharaoh's daughter; then he brought her to the city of David until he had finished building his own house, and the house of the Lord, and the wall all around Jerusalem" (1 Kings 3:1).

A similar command is given to Christians in 2 Corinthians 6:14, which reads: "Do not be unequally yoked together with unbelievers. For what fellowship has righteousness with lawlessness? And what communion has light with darkness?"

You will see how Solomon violated his own principles of decision making by marrying Pharaoh's daughter. I see patients in my practice every week whose lives are miserable because of a relationship with an unbeliever. It saddens me a great deal. This is not God's plan for His children.

Even after Solomon married Pharaoh's daughter, God still appeared to him in a dream and granted him his great wisdom.

The Lord appeared to Solomon again after he dedicated the temple. God promised to bless Solomon for obedience to His commandments, but severe consequences for turning away and worshipping other gods. I believe the Lord was giving Solomon a final warning when He appeared to him the second time with these words: "Then they will answer, 'Because they forsook the LORD their God, who brought their fathers out of the land of Egypt, and have embraced other gods, and worshiped them and served them; therefore the LORD has brought all this calamity on them'" (1 Kings 9:9).

The day finally came when Solomon's foreign wives and concubines turned his heart away from the Lord to other gods. Solomon crossed the line as far as God was concerned. He made a single poor decision that would cost him dearly. In 1 Kings 11:1–4 we read:

> *King Solomon loved many foreign women, as well as the daughter of Pharaoh: women of the Moabites, Ammonites, Edomites, Sidonians, and Hittites— from the nations of whom the LORD had said to the children of Israel, "You shall not intermarry with them, nor they with you. Surely they will turn away your hearts after their gods." Solomon clung to these in love. And he had seven hundred wives, princesses, and three hundred concubines; and his wives turned away his heart. For it was so, when Solomon was old, that his wives turned his heart after other gods; and his heart was not loyal to the LORD his God, as was the heart of his father David.*

The poor decision to marry foreign women was the beginning of Solomon's downfall. Solomon broke the first and greatest commandment. He stopped worshipping the Lord God and turned to the foreign gods worshipped by his wives. Continuing in 1 Kings 11:5–8, we read:

> *Solomon went after Ashtoreth the goddess of the Sidonians, and after Milcom the abomination of the Ammonites. Solomon did evil in the sight of the LORD, and did not fully follow the LORD, as did his father David. Then Solomon built a high place for Chemosh the abomination of Moab, on the hill that is east of Jerusalem, and for Molech the abomination of the people of Ammon. And he did likewise for all his foreign wives, who burned incense and sacrificed to their gods.*

The worship of Molech was particularly horrific, involving child sacrifice. The Lord God judged Solomon for his idolatry, tearing the kingdom from his hands. Reading from 1 Kings 11:11–12:

> *The LORD said to Solomon, "Because you have done this, and have not kept My covenant and My statutes, which I have commanded you, I will surely tear the kingdom away from you and give it to your servant. Nevertheless, I will not do it in your days, for the sake of your father David; I will tear it out of the hand of your son."*

Disobedience to God's Word cost Solomon dearly. What so often happens is that if we do not evaluate a poor decision, it will lead to a series of poor decisions. This happened with David and Bathsheba, as well as Solomon and his wives. When you realize you've made an unwise choice, do you stop and evaluate your mistake?

8. *The Lord raised up adversaries against Solomon.*

God raised up several adversaries against Solomon after he decided to worship other gods. These men were Hedad the Edomite, Rezon, and Jeroboam. These men would challenge Solomon's leadership for the rest of his days.

The consequences of bad decisions are like the turbulence on a plane ride. It is distracting, unpleasant, and makes the journey less enjoyable. Solomon's troubles could have been avoided.

9. *Solomon tried to kill God's choice for his replacement.*

Jeroboam was described as an industrious, mighty man of valor. Solomon made him the officer over the labor force of the house of Joseph. One day Jeroboam met the prophet Ahijah out in a field. Ahijah told Jeroboam that one day he would rule over ten tribes of Israel due to Solomon's idolatry. When Solomon learned about this, he tried to kill Jeroboam, much like Saul tried to kill Solomon's father David. "Solomon therefore sought to kill Jeroboam. But Jeroboam arose and fled to Egypt, to Shishak king of Egypt, and was in Egypt until the death of Solomon" (1 Kings 11:40).

Solomon's persecution of Jeroboam is the last thing we read before the great king's death and burial. What a sad ending for the wisest man who ever lived! Solomon started strong in life but finished poorly. He had the greatest insight into the decision-making process of any man in history, and yet for all his ability he made some terrible choices.

WHY BOTHER, LORD?

I did much soul searching when I began meditating on Solomon's life. If Solomon failed miserably at the end of his life, how could I or anyone else avoid doing the same? Was finishing strong as a Christian just a shot in the dark, the luck of the draw, or whatever you want to call it? No person had ever answered these questions to my satisfaction.

There is an abundance of teaching on faith. If you ask Christians what faith is, many of them would probably quote this scripture from Hebrews 11:1: "Faith is the substance of things hoped for, the evidence of things not seen." When it comes to wisdom, however, you may hear things like, "You need to use wisdom," with no further explanation on *how* to do that. I believe the reason for this is that most people only have a *general*, and not *specific*, understanding of what wisdom is.

Since nobody had really answered the questions in my heart, I took them straight to the Lord. I overcame many obstacles in order to be a physician and lieutenant colonel in the army. Up until that time, I had seemingly defeated every challenge life had thrown at me. I needed to know how I could finish life strong as a Christian if Solomon, the wisest man ever, failed miserably. I reasoned that if finishing strong in life as a Christian was just a shot in the dark, then why bother trying? I needed answers for these questions from the Lord.

The Lord loves conversing with His children. In Isaiah 1:18, one of my favorite passages of scripture, He says, "Come now, and let us reason together." I was, in effect, reasoning with my heavenly Father. I knew He had the answer. I wish I could tell you He instantly downloaded the principles I am sharing with you in this book, but it took time. The Lord did a work in me with His message before He would allow me the privilege of sharing it with you.

Speaking from Experience

What follows is a case study of sorts. My friends Ken and Carole Short learned the value of the 7 Steps to decision making first hand. This is their story.

My wife, Carole, and I founded International Data Solutions, Inc. (IDSI) in 1986, with the intention of offering data and information solutions to our clients. These services included consulting, data entry, business process outsourcing, document imaging, indexing, data mining, and medical transcription. We envisioned our clients as publishers, software developers, and companies needing help organizing , supporting, or capturing data. We had considerable expertise using related technologies and database architectures, so our focus was on the difficult and challenging task of solving our clients' data and document problems.

IDSI did well. With God's help, we succeeded despite recessions, serious competitors, and limited resources. God had blessed us with excellent partners, clients, employees, and vendors. Nevertheless, one day in 2004 I felt the Lord was saying that He would help us grow our company by as much as five times if we would trust Him. Carole and I gladly accepted the challenge. We did continue to grow, but in 2008 we encountered a major obstacle. We could not grow more without investing in a completely new office building that would cost more than a million dollars in the worst recession since the Great Depression.

Before proceeding, we met with Dr. Tillotson, and he shared with us the seven steps of the Decision Triangle and the risks of certain types of decisions. As he explained the process, Carole and I began to understand how knowledge, wisdom, faith in God, and the leading of the Holy Spirit all worked together to produce a wise outcome.

Carole and I sought the Lord's help and He reminded us that He had previously told us to "do our homework" and then pray for His direction. He had also told us to stop asking Him to bless what we do and instead trust Him to lead us as we do what He blesses. The seven steps we learned from Dr. Tillotson was the next step.

I put on my MBA hat and we quickly accomplished the first three steps of the Decision Triangle Process:

Step #1: Learning from Personal Successes and Mistakes

Step #2: Learning from Others' Successes and Mistakes

Step #3: Learning from Technical Knowledge

We then had to decide whether to proceed further in such a difficult economy. We were concerned that moving forward at that time could mean delays and eventually having to pull back. We had reached the "line of demarcation" and were about to move from one level of knowledge to another. We moved forward to the next steps:

Step #4: Learning from Wise Counsel

Step #5: Learning from the Word of God

Step #6: Learning from the Holy Spirit

After seeking out wise godly counsel, searching God's Word prayerfully, and receiving revelation knowledge from the Holy Spirit, we arrived at the last step:

Step #7: The Point of Decision

We were confident about making the decision to move forward, even though we knew that like Christopher Columbus, there would be no turning back without catastrophic consequences.

We encountered many challenges as the process continued: obtaining funding, approvals from the city, approvals from the bank, a continuing downturn in the national economy, and finding a way to serve our clients with excellence while the construction was underway. Even the weather was an issue, but God was faithful. He provided what we needed at each step along the way. Our contractor was a godly man with a godly crew working under him. We prayed for them and with them and God blessed their work. There were no accidents or injuries, and no missteps between workers and suppliers.

Carole and I agree that the beauty of these decision-making principles is the balance of faith and wisdom. We had no fear that God would change His mind or abandon us, because we were standing firmly on the promises in God's Word. We were successful in completing God's plan for us, because "we did what God blessed."

We are grateful to Dr. Tillotson for sharing the seven steps of decision making he received from God, and we know it will be beneficial to you as you make important decisions for your life.

Ken and Carole Short

DISCUSSION

1. Who does the Bible say is the wisest man who ever lived?

2. How did Jesus attest to the wisdom of Solomon in the Scriptures?

3. Why would the queen of Sheba travel so far to hear the wisdom of Solomon?

4. Name some of Solomon's successes and failures.

5. Explain the following statements:

   - In order to grow in wisdom you have to invest of your time, energy, and resources.

   - In order to grow in wisdom you have to operate in humility.

   - The primary purpose of wisdom is to help others.

   - Acquiring wisdom is an investment, not an expense.

CHAPTER 5

The King and the Valley

The wealthy king of a vast empire had two sons. One day he called his sons to him and announced that they were making a journey together to a remote valley. It took the king and his sons two weeks to arrive at their destination. Gazing out over the valley, the king pointed out a mountain that dominated the landscape near the center of the valley.

"The valley you see before you is part of my vast kingdom," the king told his sons. "I have divided it into four sections: northwest, northeast, southwest, and southeast. I am giving each of you one section of the valley on which to build your own kingdoms. Tell me which sections you will choose."

The eldest son, Eliab, stepped forward immediately. He was a tall, handsome, and physically strong man.

"I will take the southwestern portion of the valley," he told his father. "It is conveniently located close to the capital city."

"Are you sure?" his father asked.

"Yes, I'm quite sure," Eliab answered.

"What about you?" the king asked his younger son, Samuel.

"Father, might I have thirty days to make up my mind?" Samuel asked.

The king smiled and agreed to his younger son's request.

Eliab, with a satisfied grin on his face, headed back to the capital city with his father, the king, and their entourage. But Samuel, travel sack on his back and walking stick in his hand, set out alone for the center of the valley.

It took Samuel two days to reach the foot of the mountain in the center of the valley. He camped one night on the mountain and reached the summit on the second day. From his lofty vantage point, the king's younger son was able to survey the entire valley. When he had seen enough, he proceeded back down the mountain and headed back to the capital city.

On the thirtieth day, Samuel reached the gates of the city and headed straight for his father's palace. The residents of the city, having heard of the young prince's adventure, looked on with curiosity and respect as Samuel neared his destination.

The palace was full of people as the king's son entered the throne room, his rod in his hand. The king, sitting on his throne conducting business, looked up and smiled as he entered.

"Let's see what my son Samuel has to say," the king said to Eliab, who was sitting by his side. He raised his hand and his wise men, nobles, and subjects fell silent. The king rose to his feet and embraced his younger son. "I'm overjoyed to see you," he said to Samuel. "Have you decided what section of the valley you wish to take for your own?"

"Yes, Father, I have," Samuel said, smiling confidently. Then with every eye fixed on him, the young prince continued.

"After you and Eliab left for the capital, I walked two days' journey to the foot of the mountain that stands in the center of the valley. It took me two days to climb to the peak, but once I reached the summit, I was able to see the entire valley.

"This is what I discovered: The northeastern section has a few streams but many rocky and dry places not suitable for much of anything. The southeastern section is made up primarily of inhospitable desert. The southwestern section, chosen by my brother, Eliab, is mainly marsh land and swamps."

Eliab's jaw dropped suddenly, while smiles and soft laughter could be heard through the palace hall.

"The northwestern section, however, has an abundance of rivers, lakes, forests, and pastures," Samuel continued. "It is a land of great beauty and diversity. So if it agrees with you, Father, I would like the northwestern section of the valley."

"It is done as you ask," the king answered.

A roar of approval went up throughout the throne room. When it was finally quiet, Samuel addressed the king again.

"Father, if I have found favor in your eyes, could I also have the mountain that is in the center of the valley?" Samuel asked.

The king, though surprised by the request, smiled broadly. "A wise person knows when to ask for something," he answered. "The mountain is yours. Do you have a name for it?"

Samuel, who would one day sit on his father's throne, answered, "Yes, my lord, I have named it Mount Perspective. I have learned that if you wish to operate in wisdom, you need a higher perspective."

In order to stand on the mountain peak called Wisdom

where the clouds dwell, the eagles soar, and the view is the most spectacular, you must begin climbing the mountain of Knowledge at its base.

DISCUSSION

The Lord gave me the parable of "The King and the Valley" to illustrate the principles of decision making. The king is God the Father. The city and empire are the heavenly city and kingdom of heaven. The great valley is your life on earth. The eldest son, Eliab, represents pride and overconfidence. The younger son, Samuel, represents wisdom and humility. Samuel's rod is the Word of God. His sack contains acquired knowledge. His climb up the mountain represents the investment of time, energy, and resources needed to grow in wisdom. The mountain is the range of acquired knowledge. The mountain peak is the point of decision. The view from the mountain peak is perspective. The celebration in the palace signifies your blessings on earth and rewards in heaven when you operate in wisdom.

1. How does the parable of "The King and the Valley" help you understand wisdom?

2. Explain how operating in wisdom has eternal significance.

3. Name some parables Jesus used in the Bible to teach wisdom.

4. Explain how this story will help you when making decisions.

CHAPTER 6

Wisdom: The Biblical Decision-Making Process

There are many scriptures that point to the fact that we are living in the last days, or *latter times*, before Christ's return. I find being a Christian in the eleventh hour of the church both exciting and a great responsibility. There is much that the church needs to accomplish in a short period of time before Jesus returns. Christians are to do this despite the deceiving spirits and doctrines of demons that are in the world. Take a look at these three scriptures:

The Spirit expressly says that in latter times some will depart from the faith, giving heed to deceiving spirits and doctrines of demons,—1 Timothy 4:1

When the enemy comes in like a flood, the Spirit of the Lord will lift up a standard against him.—Isaiah 59:19

Wisdom and knowledge will be the stability of your times.—Isaiah 33:6

The Bible also tells us in Ephesians 5:27 that Jesus plans to present to Himself a church that is without spot or wrinkle:

"That He might present her to Himself a glorious church, not having spot or wrinkle or any such thing, but that she should be holy and without blemish." Faith that is tempered by wisdom is the key to victory in this day and hour.

WISDOM IS A PROCESS.

You have to be able to define wisdom if you are going to operate in wisdom. This is a simple but essential concept. You can only operate in wisdom to the degree that you adhere to the definition of wisdom. Let me give you an illustration. I practice obstetrical medicine. Obstetrics is the medical care of the pregnancy condition in women. This is a definition of obstetrics. If I deviate from this definition of obstetrics, I am no longer practicing obstetrics. Let's say I try to repair a leg fracture. I am no longer practicing obstetrics but orthopedics. Wisdom is the same way. If you deviate from the definition of wisdom you are no longer operating in wisdom.

The Lord gave me an illustration to help bring understanding of this concept. Picture yourself standing in front of two people. One speaks only English. The other person speaks both English and Spanish. You order the English-speaking person to "saltar." The English-speaking person is unable to do so because he does not know what "saltar" means. He just stands there. Now you tell the bilingual person to "saltar," and he begins to jump up and down. Now you instruct the English-speaking person to "saltar," and he also jumps up and down because he now knows it means to jump or leap. The English-speaking person is now able to do this *because he now knows what the word means.*

Wisdom works the same way. *If you are going to operate in wisdom in the way God intended, you have to know what God means by wisdom.*

In the remainder of this chapter, we will be exploring three definitions of wisdom:

• the English definition

• the Hebrew definition

• the scriptural definition from Proverbs 15:31–33

The scriptural definition of wisdom, very similar to the English and Hebrew, will be the definition used from this point on. We will move step by step through the process of wise decision making as the Lord has shared with me. This process is easy to learn and implement in any area of life. Even a child can learn these principles. Isn't it just like God to make things so simple and beautiful?

Learning the biblical decision-making process is similar to learning how to drive a car or ride a bike. Once you learn, you never forget. It then merely becomes a matter of perfecting your skills.

Good decision making is a methodical, step-by-step process. It is not a shot in the dark or an obscure gift that only some people can obtain. Good decision making, like faith, is something that can be developed over time, eliminating much of the guesswork and anxiety that comes with it. Using these principles is both exciting and rewarding. Rather than dreading the decision-making process, you will begin to look forward to it.

Before we look at the definition of wisdom, let's consider some of the reasons people make poor decisions.

People do not make poor decisions because of a lack of knowledge, anointing, or good intentions. People make poor decisions because of a faulty decision-making process.

The Underlying Condition

The root of poor decisions is a faulty decision-making process. It is an *underlying condition* that already exists in a person's thinking. Like a gap in a soldier's armor it can be lethal once exposed to our very real enemy —the devil. Sadly, many people are walking around with gaps in their armor and are not even aware of it!

Let's illustrate this by looking at it in a medical context. When a person has a lethal heart attack, you will often hear something like, "That person was so young and yet died of a heart attack." The heart attack was not an isolated incident. Though it may have seemed like it happened out of the blue, it was actually just a manifestation of an *underlying condition*, such as severely blocked coronary arteries. A faulty decision-making process is liked blocked coronary arteries. The signs are not always visible, but the blocked coronaries are there nonetheless. It's just a manner of time before they manifest in the form of a heart attack, some with devastating consequences.

Follow as we break down the decision-making process into its most basic component parts and then take you through the seven steps in making a wise decision. In this way, you will be able to identify, and hopefully eliminate, gaps in your decision-making armor.

A RECIPE FOR SUCCESS

My favorite cake is pineapple upside down cake. When I taste a great pineapple upside down cake, I know that someone used the right ingredients and followed the recipe. The Lord has given us a great decision-making recipe. He wants us to have great results every time we use His ingredients and follow His recipe.

WISDOM: ENGLISH, HEBREW, AND SCRIPTURAL

The *Webster's New Explorer College Dictionary* defines the noun *wisdom* as follows:

(1) accumulated learning: knowledge; (2) the ability to discern inner qualities and relationships: insight; (3) good sense: judgment; (4) a wise attitude, belief, or course of action.

Vine's Concise Dictionary of the Bible defines wisdom from the Hebrew primarily through two words:

The first is an adjective, *chakam* (Strong's # 2450), meaning "wise; skillful; practical." *Chakam* in secular usage signified a man who was a "skillful" craftsman. The manufacturers of the objects belonging to the tabernacle were known to be wise or experienced in their crafts. (See Exodus 36:1–5.)

Based on the characterization of wisdom as a skill, a class of counselors known as "wise men" arose. They were to be found in Egypt (Genesis 41:8), Babylon (Jeremiah 50:35), Tyre (Ezekiel 27:9), Edom (Obadiah 8), and Israel.

The definition of the word *chakam* would indicate that the endowment of talents is an aspect of God's wisdom. Great musicians, writers, athletes, leaders, and scientists are all expressions of this aspect of God's wisdom. The New King James translation uses the word *gifted* instead of *wise* in Exodus 36:1: "Bezalel and Aholiab, and every gifted artisan in whom the LORD has put wisdom and understanding, to know how to do all manner of work for the service of the sanctuary, shall do according to all that the LORD has commanded."

The second word for wisdom from the Hebrew is a noun, *chokmah* (Strong's #2451), meaning "wisdom; experience; shrewdness." *Chokmah* is the knowledge and ability to make right choices at the opportune time. Consistently making right choices is an indication of maturity and development. The prerequisite for "wisdom" is the fear of the Lord. In simple terms, the Hebrew word for wisdom means the ability to make good decisions.

The *ability* to make good decisions is a *process*. If the Hebrew word for wisdom means the ability to make good decisions, and ability is a process, then wisdom means the process of making good decisions.

This brings us to the scriptural definition of wisdom.

This is how the biblical decision-making process found in Proverbs 15:31–33 is supposed to work. First, let's look at the scripture itself: "The ear that hears the rebukes of life will abide among the wise. He who disdains instruction despises his own soul, but he who heeds rebuke gets understanding. The fear of the LORD is the instruction of wisdom, and before honor is humility."

This passage of scripture defines wisdom as a range of acquired knowledge that is rightly applied.

Wisdom has two parts:

Part 1: *a range of acquired knowledge* (the knowledge acquired in making a decision)

Part 2: *right application* (determines what makes a decision wise)

Wisdom = Range of Acquired Knowledge + Right Application

You alone will decide how this will change your decision-making process. Proverbs 18:15 says: "The heart of the prudent acquires knowledge, and the ear of the wise seeks knowledge."

Part 1: A Range of Acquired Knowledge

The first part of operating in wisdom is to have a *range of acquired knowledge*. Let's begin by discussing the word *acquired*.

You cannot operate in wisdom you do not have. For example, you cannot operate in wisdom someone else has unless you have acquired the knowledge from that person. I know quite a bit about surgery, but I know very little about automobiles. For me to have the knowledge of a mechanic, I have to invest time, energy, and resources to acquire that knowledge. Only then am I able to operate in wisdom in that area. You can only benefit from knowledge and wisdom you have acquired. Proverbs 9:12 says: "If you are wise, you are wise for yourself, and if you scoff, you will bear it alone."

Now we must define the word *knowledge*. *Webster's New Explorer College Dictionary* has four definitions for the word knowledge. One definition calls it the range of one's *information* or awareness. Knowledge is information. Therefore, it can be said that wisdom is a range of acquired information that is rightly applied.

When you are acquiring knowledge, you are simply gaining information. Anybody can do this. Sometimes people think they cannot have wisdom because it is beyond their capacity. Nothing could be further from the truth! If you can get information and rightly apply it, you can be as wise as anyone. There is a *range of knowledge* you can acquire to operate in greater wisdom. This range of knowledge can be explained by the following twelve rules.

Twelve Rules of Knowledge

1. There are three levels of knowledge: observation, education, and revelation.

2. *Observation* is the lowest, *education* the middle, and *revelation* the highest level of knowledge.

3. Each level of knowledge has two categories for a total of six categories of knowledge.

4. Each level and category of knowledge builds on the preceding level and category.

5. Non-Christians can only operate in the three lowest categories of knowledge, while Christians have the capability of operating in all six categories.

6. How much knowledge you need from a particular category will be determined by the kind of decision you are making: (1) a daily living decision; (2) an ethical decision; (3) a goal-oriented decision.

7. People usually make poor decisions because they are lacking in one or more of the six categories of knowledge.

8. The higher the level of knowledge you desire, the more time, energy, and resources you will have to invest to acquire it.

9. Humility, like strength, enables you to climb the mountain of knowledge.

10. Pride, like gravity, prevents you from climbing the mountain of knowledge.

11. The greater the amount of knowledge you have acquired, the easier and more beneficial a decision becomes.

12. There are seven steps in making a wise decision that is based on knowledge.

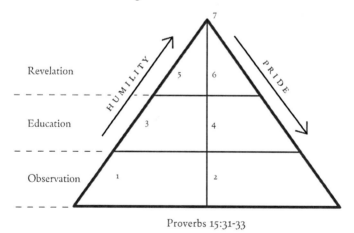

Proverbs 15:31-33

In this chapter, we discussed the meaning of wisdom and twelve rules that govern knowledge. In the chapters that follow, we will work through the biblical decision-making process one step at a time. Are you ready to go mountain climbing?

In order to stand on the mountain peak called Wisdom where the clouds dwell, the eagles soar, and the view is the most spectacular, you must begin climbing the mountain of Knowledge at its base.

DISCUSSION

1. Explain the following statement from this chapter: "People do not make poor decisions because of a lack of knowledge, anointing, or good intentions. People make poor decisions because of a faulty decision-making process."

2. A faulty decision-making process was described as both a gap in a soldier's armor and blocked coronary arteries. Explain. Give some other examples to illustrate a faulty decision-making process.

3. True or false:

   - In simple terms, the Hebrew word for wisdom means the ability to make good decisions.

   - Wisdom means the process of making good decisions.

   - Wisdom is available for only a chosen few. You either have it or you don't.

   - Wisdom is a range of acquired knowledge that is rightly applied.

   - You can only benefit from knowledge and wisdom you have acquired.

4. Fill in the blank.

- Wisdom = Range of Acquired Knowledge + _____ _____.

5. Read through The Twelve Rules of Knowledge in this chapter. What are the three levels of knowledge based on Proverbs 15:31–33?

6. Look at the diagram for the biblical decision-making process at the end of the chapter. Practice drawing the diagram from memory until you have learned it.

CHAPTER 7

Observation: The First Level of Knowledge

Proverbs 15:31–33 is the foundational passage for this teaching on decision making. Each verse makes reference to one of the three levels of knowledge. Verse 31 speaks about the first level of knowledge, that is, *observation* knowledge. This is knowledge gained by experience. "The ear that hears the rebukes of life will abide among the wise" (Proverbs 15:31).

Observation knowledge is knowledge gained through observation of life experiences. We can break it down into the first two categories of knowledge or learning:

Category #1: Learning from personal successes and mistakes

Category #2: Learning from the successes and mistakes of others

Of the three levels of knowledge, observation knowledge is the easiest to acquire. It requires the smallest investment of time, energy, and resources. You can learn from your life experiences and those of others wherever you go.

Genesis 30–31 tells the story of Jacob and his wives dwelling in the land with Laban, his uncle. Jacob was ready to return to his own country after having served Laban for many years, but

Laban had other ideas. He had learned by experience that God was with Jacob, the source of his prosperity. Genesis 30:25–27 says:

> *It came to pass, when Rachel had borne Joseph, that Jacob said to Laban, "Send me away, that I may go to my own place and to my country. Give me my wives and my children for whom I have served you, and let me go; for you know my service which I have done for you." And Laban said to him, "Please stay, if I have found favor in your eyes, for I have learned by experience that the LORD has blessed me for your sake."*

A person with humility will learn from observation knowledge, but a person who is full of pride is not capable of learning at this lowest level of knowledge. Do you remember the twelve rules of knowledge in chapter 6? Rules 9 and 10 deal with humility and pride, respectively.

9. Humility, like strength, enables you to climb the mountain of knowledge.

10. Pride, like gravity, prevents you from climbing the mountain of knowledge.

In the parable of the king and the valley, Samuel represents humility and Eliab represents pride. The issue of humility versus pride is fundamental when learning how to operate in wisdom. Humility versus pride is mentioned at each level of knowledge in Proverbs 15:31–33. Read these verses carefully. You will see that humility is a prerequisite for acquiring each level of knowledge, while pride prevents you from doing so.

Observation Knowledge:

> *The ear that hears the rebukes of life will abide among the wise.*—Proverbs 15:31

Education Knowledge:

> *He who disdains instruction despises his own soul, but he who heeds rebuke gets understanding.*—Proverbs 15:32

Revelation Knowledge:

> *The fear of the LORD is the instruction of wisdom, and before honor is humility.*—Proverbs 15:33

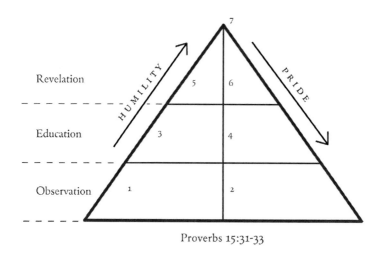

Proverbs 15:31-33

Humility

Webster's College Dictionary describes a humble person as someone who is modest, meek, and unpretentious. In other words, someone who is teachable and doesn't think he knows it all. Humble people are quick learners. They are continually growing. There is no limit to how far they can go in God.

- **Humble people listen to godly instruction.** Proverbs 1:8–9 says: "My son, hear the instruction of your father, and do not forsake the law of your mother; for they will be a graceful ornament on your head, and chains about your neck."

- **Humble people value instruction.** They have an earnest desire to grow in discernment and understanding. Humble people reverence God and His Word. Proverbs 2:1–5 says: "My son, if you receive my words, and treasure my commands within you, so that you incline your ear to wisdom, and apply your heart to understanding; yes, if you cry out for discernment, and lift up your voice for understanding, if you seek her as silver, and search for her as for hidden treasures; then you will understand the fear of the LORD, and find the knowledge of God."

- **Humble people conduct themselves with discretion.** Proverbs 3:21–22 says: "My son, let them not depart from your eyes—keep sound wisdom and discretion; so they will be life to your soul and grace to your neck."

- **Humble people acquire and retain knowledge.** Proverbs 5:1–2 says: "My son, pay attention to my wisdom; lend your ear to my understanding, that you may preserve discretion, and your lips may keep knowledge."

- **Jesus is our example of humility.** A humble person will grow in wisdom, stature, and favor with God and man.

Luke 2:52 says: "Jesus increased in wisdom and stature, and in favor with God and men."

Pride

Webster's College Dictionary defines pride as excessive self-esteem: conceit. A person full of pride thinks he or she is better than others or knows more than everyone else. This is why proud people won't grow in knowledge. They think they already know it all.

The one thing a mountain climber has to continually overcome is the force of gravity. Pride works like gravity. You have to continually overcome pride if you are going to go up in your level of knowledge and wisdom. The higher up the mountain you go, the more it will cost you to remain teachable.

- **Proud people won't listen to reason, and harm themselves in the process.** They prefer destruction over wisdom. Proverbs 8:34–36 says: "Blessed is the man who listens to me, watching daily at my gates, waiting at the posts of my doors. For whoever finds me finds life, and obtains favor from the Lord; but he who sins against me wrongs his own soul; all those who hate me love death."

- **Proud people won't receive instruction or correction.** Therefore, they will inevitably go astray. Proverbs 10:17 says: "He who keeps instruction is in the way of life, but he who refuses correction goes astray."

- **Proud people don't dislike correction, they hate it!** The Bible calls a person who hates correction stupid. Proverbs

12:1 says: "Whoever loves instruction loves knowledge, but he who hates correction is stupid."

- **Proud people are always headed for a fall.** Proverbs 16:18 says: "Pride goes before destruction and a haughty spirit before a fall."

- **A proud person is wise in his own eyes.** Proverbs 26:12 says: "Do you see a man wise in his own eyes? There is more hope for a fool than for him.

- **It is easier to crush grain in a mortar than grind the foolishness out of a proud person.** Proverbs 27:22 says: "Though you grind a fool in a mortar with a pestle along with crushed grain, yet his foolishness will not depart from him."

- **God Himself resists, or opposes, the proud person.** When he humbles himself, however, God's grace is made available. James 4:6 says: "God resists the proud, but gives grace to the humble."

Pride led to the fall of Satan, the devil. His plan is to entangle people in pride so they will fall just like he did. Pride is easy to spot; it is always *I* centered. Don't let the devil get you into I-centered thinking, speaking, or decision making. Isaiah 14:12–15 says:

How you are fallen from heaven, O Lucifer, son of the morning! How you are cut down to the ground, you who weakened the nations! For you have said in your heart: "I will ascend into heaven, I will exalt my throne above the stars of God; I will also sit on the mount of the congregation on the farthest sides of the north; I will ascend above the heights of the clouds, I will be like the Most High." Yet you shall be brought down to Sheol, to the lowest depths of the Pit.

Now you are ready to explore the two steps for obtaining observation knowledge.

STEP #1: LEARNING FROM PERSONAL SUCCESSES AND MISTAKES

The ear that hears the rebukes of life will abide among the wise.—Proverbs 15:31

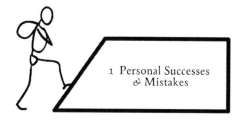

Learning from personal successes and mistakes is the most basic and lowest category of knowledge. Until you have mastered this category there will be problems down the road, because your foundation is unstable. Learning from personal successes is learning things the easy way. Learning from personal mistakes is learning things the hard way. Both are beneficial, but learning from your mistakes is more painful and costly. We are supposed to learn from our successes and mistakes regardless of whether we are making daily living, ethical, or goal-oriented decisions. This is the most elementary step of growing in wisdom.

Learning from Personal Successes

Let's look again at Genesis 30:27: "Laban said to him, "Please stay, if I have found favor in your eyes, for *I have learned by experience that the* LORD *has blessed me for your sake.*" In this story of Jacob and Laban, there comes a point where Laban realizes he is prospering because God's hand is on his nephew. He does everything he can to get Jacob to stay with him.

In 1 Samuel 23:1–5, we see how David learned by experience that inquiring of the Lord before going into battle was a formula for success:

> *Then they told David, saying, "Look, the Philistines are fighting against Keilah, and they are robbing the threshing floors." Therefore David inquired of the* LORD, *saying, "Shall I go and attack these Philistines?" And the* LORD *said to David, "Go and attack the Philistines, and save Keilah." But David's men said to him, "Look, we are afraid here in Judah. How much more then if we go to Keilah against the armies of the Philistines?" Then David inquired of the Lord once again. And the* LORD *answered him and said, "Arise, go down to Keilah. For I will deliver the Philistines into your hand." And David and his men went to Keilah and fought with the Philistines, struck them with a mighty blow, and took away their livestock. So David saved the inhabitants of Keilah.*

David's success at Keilah would serve him well later on. One day the Amalekites attacked David's base at Ziklag while he and his men were away. They burned Ziklag to the ground and took all the women and children captive. Some of David's men were speaking of stoning him because of their grief! In 1 Samuel 30:6–8 we read:

> *David strengthened himself in the LORD his God. Then David said to Abiathar the priest, Ahimelech's son, "Please bring the ephod here to me." And Abiathar brought the ephod to David. So David inquired of the LORD, saying, "Shall I pursue this troop? Shall I overtake them?" And He answered him, "Pursue, for you shall surely overtake them and without fail recover all.*

David did not hesitate once he heard God give him the word to pursue the Amalekites. He had learned from personal success that he could trust God. He and his men eventually caught up with the enemy and attacked them. They recovered everything, just as God had spoken. "Nothing of theirs was lacking, either small or great, sons or daughters, spoil or anything which they had taken from them; David recovered all" (1 Samuel 30:19).

Wouldn't it be nice to have an ephod like David to help you know what to do? You actually have something better! You have the Word of God that is a lamp to your feet and a light to your path. (See Psalm 119:105.)

Let me give you some examples of the value of learning from personal successes.

As an OB/GYN surgeon, I have learned the more time I spend with my patients before surgery, the more satisfied they are. When a patient comes to see me, I spend time going over the medical history and personal concerns. I spend time explaining to each patient the particulars of her medical condition in terms she can understand. I spend time answering any questions she might have. I spend time discussing medical versus surgical options. If the patient desires to proceed with surgery, I spend time discussing how the operation is performed and what the possible complications might be.

At the end of each visit I ask my patients, "Do you have any questions about what we talked about?" Rarely do patients say "yes" at this point, but if they do, I spend time answering their questions. When my patients are ready to leave, I affirm, "I'll see you the morning of surgery, and I'll be happy to answer any questions you might have before we take you to the OR." I want each of my patients to know that her surgery is important to me and that we are going into this thing together. I rarely have a dissatisfied customer. I do not deviate from this practice. I have learned to stick with what works.

The example I just gave you about preparing patients for surgery falls into the category of goal-oriented decisions. I have also learned from my successes in the area of ethical decisions.

I do not make commitments I cannot keep. If I am not able to keep my word then I have violated my integrity and my ethics. My wife used to think I didn't ever want to commit to anything. Over time she has realized that the demands on me as a physician can be significant and that balance is very important for our family. Another ethical lesson I have learned is honesty. One of the Ten Commandments is to not bear false witness or lie. We have a saying in our home, "Honesty is its own defense." Lying is never OK. This is a valuable ethical lesson that has to be learned in life.

Learning from personal successes in daily living also has great rewards.

I make it a habit when driving to put my turn signal on long before I make a turn. This gives the driver behind me time to realize I am turning, and adequate opportunity to slow down. I have taught my daughters this valuable lesson. They have seen what sometimes happens when people don't do this. I have also learned to slow down when there are snowy and icy road conditions.

I'll never forget what I saw when driving to work one winter in Oklahoma. We had about eight inches of snow on the ground from a recent storm. I was driving forty-five miles an hour on a one-way, two-lane highway. The normal speed limit for this highway was sixty five miles per hour, but because of the weather, all cars were traveling in the right-hand lane, carving a trail that other drivers were quite happy to follow for safety's sake. The only exception was the driver in the car behind me.

As I looked in my rearview mirror, I saw a blue sedan racing down the frozen fast lane at about sixty-five miles an hour. At that point, he was about fifty yards behind me and closing in fast! I was wondering what was going to happen next. I did not have to wait long. The car began to swerve out of control. He would have gone off the road into a ditch had it not been for a fortuitous segment of guard railing. The right rear of his car slammed into the railing and dented his vehicle. Only then did he slow down and get in the right lane behind the rest of us. I sighed with relief and said to myself, *That man learned a valuable lesson from his mistake.* Was I ever wrong!

A few minutes later another car decided to do what the blue sedan tried earlier. He sped right by the rest of us in the ice lane at sixty-five miles per hour. The man in the blue, now-dented vehicle wasn't going to be left behind and took off after him! That man's angel was working overtime trying to keep him alive because he refused to learn from his near fatal mistake. He was driven by pride. Proverbs 16:18 says: "Pride goes before destruction, and a haughty spirit before a fall."

Pride is something you don't play around with. One prideful act, even during a daily living decision, can be deadly. Pride has to be dealt with or it can cost you your life and destiny. This leads me to the next subject.

Learning from Personal Mistakes

In Proverbs 20:30 Solomon says: "Blows that hurt cleanse away evil, as do stripes the inner depths of the heart." He is talking here about the hard lessons of life. Only fools like to suffer unnecessarily. Perhaps you have heard the saying, "He only learns things the hard way." The reason for this is stubbornness, at the root of which is pride. *Webster's College Dictionary* defines stubborn as "hard to convince, persuade, or move to action; obstinate." Doesn't that mean someone who is unwilling to change and to learn from his or her mistakes?

I like the saying, "Wise people learn from their mistakes the first time. Fools make the same mistake twice." It challenges me to examine myself. How about you?

We all make mistakes. The test is how willing we are to learn from those mistakes and not repeat them over and over. This is

at the heart of why people do not rise to another level in knowledge and wisdom. Stubbornness and pride have to be dealt with
at every category and level of knowledge. The unwillingness
to learn and change behavior keeps people in the quagmire of
mediocrity. Paul had to deal with this issue. The Bible calls it the
carnal, or sin, nature of man. Stubbornness and pride are sins,
as we learn from Romans 7:14–19:

> *For we know that the law is spiritual, but I am carnal, sold*
> *under sin. For what I am doing, I do not understand. For what*
> *I will to do, that I do not practice; but what I hate, that I do.*
> *If, then, I do what I will not to do, I agree with the law that it*
> *is good. But now, it is no longer I who do it, but sin that dwells*
> *in me. For I know that in me (that is, in my flesh) nothing good*
> *dwells; for to will is present with me, but how to perform what*
> *is good I do not find. For the good that I will to do, I do not do;*
> *but the evil I will not to do, that I practice.*

Paul realized that he was born again, a new creation in
Christ, and yet he still had to deal with his old sin nature. Even
though he wanted to do what was right, he sometimes failed. I
think we can all understand how Paul must have felt, but there
is an answer to this problem worded so eloquently in Romans
7:24: "O wretched man that I am! Who will deliver me from
this body of death?"

The answer is Jesus Christ. In the very next verse, Romans
7:25, we read: "I thank God—through Jesus Christ our Lord!
So then, with the mind I myself serve the law of God, but with
the flesh the law of sin."

Some bad habits or mistakes are so entrenched in people's thinking that it takes a supreme act of the will, and sometimes God's grace, to change behavior. God's grace is made available to us through the redemptive work of Jesus Christ at the cross.

For example, those who are addicted to drugs or alcohol will stand a better chance of getting off and staying off those substances if they allow God's grace or ability in their lives to help them. As Christians, we have God's enabling power through Jesus Christ to help us change wrong patterns of behavior. Philippians 4:13 says: "I can do all things through Christ who strengthens me."

One of the reasons marriages fail is that one or both partners are unwilling to learn from their mistakes and change how they treat their spouse. Sometimes the Holy Spirit is needed to point things out and provide the grace to change. God's Word is also needed to renew the mind. Romans 12:2 says: "Do not be conformed to this world, but be transformed by the renewing of your mind, that you may prove what is that good and acceptable and perfect will of God."

Buddy Bear

In raising three daughters, I have had to learn to communicate with girls differently than with boys. There is a difference, let me tell you. Little girls get their feelings hurt much more easily. At first it was confusing for me because I had no experience raising girls.

When one of my girls came down with a minor illness or injury, I would check it out and announce, "You'll be OK." I thought I was doing the right thing, but my girls didn't think so. They wanted a concerned father rather than a smart doctor. They would eye me suspiciously to see if I was genuinely concerned. If I cracked a smile under their scrutiny, I knew I would be in trouble. I spent a lot of time doing damage control. My wife finally made me realize the girls just wanted me to hug them and love on them instead of giving them a "matter-of-fact" prognosis.

Now that my youngest of three girls is a teenager, I feel like an expert in this area—almost. I made some mistakes, but I decided years ago that I would learn from those mistakes in order to become a better father. The rewards have been worth the effort. One of their nicknames for me is "Buddy Bear." I like it, don't you?

Frying Fish in Hawaii

In 1999, while still in the army, I was transferred from Fort Leonard Wood, Missouri, to Tripler Army Medical Center in Honolulu, Hawaii. I had several weeks off to find a place to live and get settled in before starting work at the hospital. I had just finished a busy three-year tour of duty at an army hospital with only three OB/GYN doctors for the entire post. I was looking forward to some time off after moving our family to the middle of the Pacific and living out of suitcases.

Shortly after moving into our military quarters, I decided to fry some big fish filets, along with onions and tomatoes, just the way I like them. A little lemon juice on top would be the finishing touch. I was in the kitchen wearing a comfortable Aloha shirt with shorts and sandals. The sink was full of dishes. I had a large skillet on the front burner one inch deep in hot cooking oil. I had successfully fried a couple of filets and was on my way to preparing a sumptuous meal. I grasped a huge filet with the tongs to place in the skillet. In a moment of carelessness, I raised the filet about one foot above skillet and lost control of the fish with the grasper. The fish landed in the center of the skillet full of hot oil and created a splash that was headed right toward my abdomen!

I had only a split second to react. I pulled my abdomen back from the wave of hot oil coming at me. Unfortunately, however, my right lower leg got splattered. I had to deal with a sink full of dishes while I tried to get some cold water on my leg. I went to the emergency room and got treated for second-degree burns. Worst of all, I wasn't going to be able to go swimming in the ocean during my time off before starting work at the hospital. I was very disappointed with myself for making such a careless mistake.

Because the first category of knowledge is learning from personal successes and mistakes, I knew I had to make some changes or this kind of accident might happen again. I had an incentive to change. The thought of God rolling His eyes at me for not learning from this mistake was unacceptable. I had to change my behavior.

I have now made the following changes when I fry food. I wear a pair of jeans and tennis shoes instead of shorts and sandals. I make sure the kitchen sink is empty in case I need access to cold water. I use the back burner, which is farther away from me. I use a thin layer of oil to fry my food. I am careful not to raise the food more than a few inches above the skillet. I also wear glasses to protect my eyes, no differently than if I was doing surgery.

This all may sound silly, but this is wisdom. Learning from personal successes and mistakes is step one of wisdom. If you don't master step one, you won't be able to move on to step two. I have not been injured again like I was that day in Hawaii because I learned from my mistake. I have been tempted occasionally to cut corners on these precautions. That can be easy to do. This is where stubbornness and pride have to be eliminated. This is why some people make the same mistakes over and over. It may be subtle at times, but the underlying issue is unresolved pride, as the next story humorously illustrates.

Has Anybody Seen My Shoes?

In October of 2006, after a year of lobbying by my wife Libby and youngest daughter Rebekah, I agreed to buy a Labradoodle puppy. I had big reservations, because I have learned from experience that having a puppy is like having a baby. They require a great deal of attention. Don't get me wrong. I love dogs and enjoy doing things with them, but I had hoped this season in my life was over. I was, after all, writing a book on decision making and wasn't interested in distractions. As you have probably guessed, I caved in to wife and child.

Brownie came to live with us when she was four months old. Like any normal, playful puppy, she enjoyed taking shoes out the doggy door into the back yard. I was on to Brownie in a hurry and quickly learned that leaving my shoes lying around would be inviting disaster. I immediately put my shoes in our bedroom closet and made sure the dog did not have access to our bedroom.

My daughters had not yet learned what puppies can do. They had the habit of taking off their shoes in the den after school. It wasn't long before I started hearing, "Has anybody seen my shoes?" The girls were upset to discover their favorite shoes had become dog toys.

I tried to tell the girls to put their shoes away after school, but to no avail. I even put their shoes away myself, when I could, to avoid what was becoming an expensive problem. Periodically, however, I would hear, "Has anybody seen my shoes?" I realized the girls were going to have to learn from their mistake themselves, and I decided not to replace their favorite shoes. Whenever one of my three teenage daughters discovered Brownie chewing one of their shoes, I would kindly remind them, "Honey, remember the first level of knowledge." They knew exactly what I was talking about. Their reply would be, "Oh dad, I can't wait until Brownie gets a hold of one of *your* shoes." I could never allow that to happen. If Brownie got hold of one of my shoes, I knew I would be hearing "Dad, remember the first level of knowledge" the rest of my life.

This cycle of discovery and instruction went on for a couple of weeks until the girls started going to school in their worn-out shoes. They finally decided it was better to learn from their mistakes than to pay the price for repeating them. We all laugh about it to this day.

MODEL OF EFFICIENCY

A lifestyle of learning from your mistakes is invaluable. As an obstetrician and surgeon, I am constantly evaluating myself and eliminating any practice or surgical technique that does not provide the best patient care. As a result of this, I encounter few problems in my practice. I have a great deal of personal and patient satisfaction. I enjoy good relationships with the nursing and clerical staff that I work with. Purposefully learning from and eliminating mistakes has helped me become a better physician. This principle will work in any area of your life if you are willing to humble yourself and learn.

David and Samson

Let's take a moment to contrast the experiences of David and Samson. One learned from his mistakes in personal relationships and one did not.

When Nathan the prophet confronted David about his sin with Bathsheba, David immediately acknowledged his sin. In 2 Samuel 12:13 we read: "David said to Nathan, 'I have sinned against the LORD.' And Nathan said to David, 'The LORD also has put away your sin; you shall not die.'"

In most cases, a poor ethical decision is sin. When God's people sin, many people are affected. The higher the position of leadership and influence a person has, the greater the degree of damage their sin causes. David's sin in the matter of Uriah and Bathsheba affected God Himself. In 2 Samuel 11:27 we read: "The thing that David had done displeased the Lord."

David's behavior lowered his standard in the eyes of his family, servants, and nation. The child conceived in adultery died. His sin also gave his enemies an opportunity to reproach him.

God, in His mercy, forgave David when he repented. David's sin, however, gave God's enemies an occasion to blaspheme Him. "Because by this deed you have given great occasion to the enemies of the LORD to blaspheme" (2 Samuel 12:14).

David genuinely repented of his sin. He did not commit adultery again. Psalm 51 was written by David and gives us insight into his deep remorse. Let's read verses 1–4:

Have mercy upon me, O God, according to Your lovingkindness; according to the multitude of Your tender mercies, blot out my transgressions. Wash me thoroughly from my iniquity, and cleanse me from my sin. For I acknowledge my transgressions, and my sin is always before me. Against You, You only, have I sinned, and done this evil in Your sight.

David continues his discourse in Psalm 51:10–12: "Create in me a clean heart, O God, and renew a steadfast spirit within me. Do not cast me away from Your presence, and do not take Your Holy Spirit from me. Restore to me the joy of Your salvation, and uphold me by Your generous Spirit."

The first part of Romans 6:23 tells us that the wages of sin is death. Nathan the prophet said one last thing to David before leaving his presence. "However, because by this deed you have given great occasion to the enemies of the LORD to blaspheme, the child also who is born to you shall surely die" (2 Samuel 12:14).

David fasted and prayed for a week, but the child still died. "David arose from the ground, washed and anointed himself, and changed his clothes; and he went into the house of the LORD and worshiped. Then he went to his own house; and when he requested, they set food before him, and he ate" (2 Samuel 12:20).

David learned a hard and painful lesson from his sin. He was restored to God because he humbled himself, repented, and learned from his mistakes. Samson, however, did not learn from his mistakes so easily and paid a heavy price.

Before there were kings in Israel, the nation was led by a series of God-appointed judges. Samson was one of these and he judged Israel for twenty years. His story is found in Judges chapters 13 to 16. Chapter 14 tells the story of Samson's disastrous marriage to a daughter of the Philistines despite his parents' advice and God's commandment against such a union. In a bout of rage during the wedding feast, Samson killed thirty Philistine men and returned to his father's house. Samson's wife was then given to his best man. What a mess!

It gets worse.

Samson eventually tried to see his Philistine wife, and when he discovered that she had been given to his best man, he went into a rage. In retaliation, he set fire to the grain fields, vineyards, and olive groves of the Philistines. The Philistines then set fire to Samson's wife and her father. He had now become a wanted man, and the Philistines were determined to get him. Samson then killed one thousand Philistines with the jawbone of a donkey. You would think that he might have learned something from his disastrous marriage, but he did not.

Samson returned to the land of the Philistines and got involved with a harlot. Samson did not learn from this sinful mistake either. He then got involved with a third woman, a Philistine named Delilah. "Afterward it happened that he loved a woman in the Valley of Sorek, whose name was Delilah" (Judges 16.4).

The lords of the Philistines paid Delilah eleven hundred pieces of silver to get her to discover the secret of his strength and betray him. Over time she gained his trust and finally got him to reveal that his great strength lay in his uncut hair as he was a Nazarite to God from his mother's womb. Samson made a fatal mistake by revealing the source of his strength. Delilah wasted no time delivering the secret to the Philistines. Judges 16:19 says: "She lulled him to sleep on her knees, and called for a man and had him shave off the seven locks of his head. Then she began to torment him and his strength left him."

When Delilah cut his hair, Samson lost the last bit of his consecration to God. When the Philistines came upon Samson this time, he did not know that the LORD had departed from him. Samson's prideful sin made him oblivious to the danger around him. "The Philistines took him and put out his eyes, and brought him down to Gaza. They bound him with bronze fetters, and he became a grinder in the prison" (Judges 16:21).

What a tragic end for the leader of a nation. Samson's captors blinded him, put him in a foreign prison, and forced him to do the work of slaves and beasts of burden. What happened to Samson is an illustration of what happens to believers when they sin. They lose their consecration, as well as their spiritual eyesight or discernment, and they open themselves up to be controlled by their enemy the devil.

There came a day when the lords of the Philistines made a celebration to Dagon their god, and Samson was to be put on display in their temple. The incident is recorded in Judges 16:23–25:

> *The lords of the Philistines gathered together to offer a great sacrifice to Dagon their god, and to rejoice. And they said: "Our god has delivered into our hands Samson our enemy!" When the people saw him, they praised their god; for they said: "Our god has delivered into our hands our enemy, the destroyer of our land, and the one who multiplied our dead." So it happened, when their hearts were merry, that they said, "Call for Samson, that he may perform for us." So they called for Samson from the prison, and he performed for them. And they stationed him between the pillars.*

The Lord showed me how this passage of scripture mirrors what goes on in the spirit realm when Christians sin. The lords of the Philistines represent the demonic principalities and powers spoken of in Ephesians 6:12. They offer up sacrifices to their god, Satan. Samson represents the believer who has fallen into the deception and bondage of sin. The demons celebrate the fact that their god, Satan, has delivered the person who sinned into their control. When believers sin, they are performing for demons, much the same way Samson was made to perform for the Philistines. The two pillars where Samson was made to stand between represent the pillars of guilt and condemnation.

Finally, Samson repented of his sin and learned from his mistakes. His hair had begun to grow back. He humbled himself and cried out to God. We read his words in Judges 16:28: "Samson called to the LORD, saying, "O Lord GOD, remember me, I pray! Strengthen me, I pray, just this once, O God, that I may with one blow take vengeance on the Philistines for my two eyes!"

Having said these words, Samson braced himself against the two pillars and Judges 16:30–31 tells us what happened next:

> *Samson said, "Let me die with the Philistines!" And he pushed with all his might, and the temple fell on the lords and all the people who were in it. So the dead that he killed at his death were more than he had killed in his life. And his brothers and all his father's household came down and took him, and brought him up and buried him between Zorah and Eshtaol in the tomb of his father Manoah. He had judged Israel twenty years.*

Samson finally humbled himself, repented, and was restored to God. Unfortunately, he learned from his mistakes too late and it cost him his eyesight and his life. However, God acknowledged his final act of bravery by including him among the heroes of faith in Hebrews chapter 11.

We've completed the first step in making a wise decision: learning from personal successes and mistakes. There are seven questions you have to ask yourself when making a wise decision.

You are now ready to answer the first question. When you have done that, you are ready to move on to Step #2.

Question #1—What have I learned from personal successes and mistakes?

Discussion

1. According to Proverbs 15:31, what is the lowest level of knowledge?

2. What are the first two categories of knowledge at this level?

3. What helps or hinders someone from growing in observation knowledge, based on the twelve rules of knowledge in chapter 6?

4. What do rules of knowledge 9 and 10 say about humility and pride?

5. True or false:

   • God resists the proud, but gives grace to the humble.

6. Compare decisions you have made in the past in pride versus humility.

7. What is the first category of knowledge and first step in making a wise decision?

8. Give some examples of times when you learned from personal successes.

9. Give some examples of times when you learned from personal mistakes.

10 Give some examples of times when you did not learn from personal successes and paid a price.

11. Give some examples of times when you did not learn from personal mistakes and paid a price.

12. Can you identify any personal mistakes you keep repeating?

13. What are you going to do to avoid making personal mistakes over and over again?

14. What is the first question you have to ask yourself in making a wise decision?

STEP #2 LEARNING FROM OTHERS' SUCCESSES AND MISTAKES

The ear that hears the rebukes of life will abide among the wise.—Proverbs 15:31

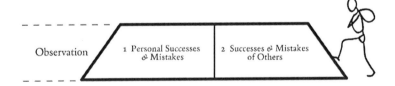

Learning from others' successes and mistakes is the second category of observation knowledge. To obtain this kind of knowledge requires that you invest a little more time, energy, and resources. You must also humble yourself and admit two things:

1. Someone else knows more about a particular subject than I do.

2. What happens to someone else, good or bad, can also happen to me.

The next couple of scriptures illustrate these two points in the areas of diligence and hard work.

> *Go to the ant, you sluggard! Consider her ways and be wise, which, having no captain, overseer or ruler, provides her supplies in the summer, and gathers her food in the harvest.*—Proverbs 6:6–8

> *The lazy man will not plow because of winter; he will beg during harvest and have nothing.*—Proverbs 20:4

Clearly this second category of knowledge—observation—includes a built-in advantage. You can learn a great deal from others' successes and mistakes without having to pay the price they had to pay for that knowledge. The question is: are you humble enough to learn from others? You can gain this kind of information primarily by two means:

1. Direct observation (basically by watching, listening, and spending time with another person)

2. Indirect observation (includes communication through media such as books, magazines, television, and radio)

Direct Observation

Direct observation is good because you can see everything that is going on. You can also gain hands-on experience in the area of knowledge you are acquiring. You are able to ask questions when you are working with and observing someone directly. The military uses this form of training. The army has a saying: "See one; do one; teach one." This principle of *see, do,* and *teach* is found in the Bible. Ezra 7:10 says: "Ezra had prepared his heart to *seek* the Law of the LORD, and to *do* it, and to *teach* statutes and ordinances in Israel."

See one, do one, teach one is a simple but useful phrase. In the army there are small publications called *Lessons Learned.* These valuable tools allow soldiers to learn from the successes and mistakes of those who have gone before them. In the United States military service academies and other schools, like the War College, studying the historical lessons of warfare is part of the curriculum.

If the military invests so much time, energy, and resources training their people for the *possibility* of war, shouldn't we as Christians be investing time, energy, and resources to be trained when we are *already* at war with demonic forces? We remember what the apostle Paul said in Ephesians 6:12: "We do not wrestle against flesh and blood, but against principalities, against powers, against the rulers of the darkness of this age, against spiritual hosts of wickedness in the heavenly places."

You may not think of yourself as a soldier, but the Bible says that Christians are soldiers in God's Army. Read 2 Timothy 2:4:

"No one engaged in warfare entangles himself with the affairs of this life, that he may please him who enlisted him as a soldier."

Believe me, when you begin to make prudent decisions and start achieving God's purposes for your life, your enemy, the devil, will engage you in warfare. You will need to think of yourself as a soldier and use God's wisdom and His Word to avoid entanglements the enemy has laid out for you like booby traps.

Indirect Observation

With the advancement of communication and technology, you can learn a great deal from other people through communication media. The more you observe, the more you learn if you become a student of life. I enjoy reading other people's biographies and autobiographies and observing how those individuals handled both adversity and success. By reading this book, you can learn from *my* mistakes and successes.

Television and movies are also useful tools for learning valuable life lessons, though a note of caution is needed here. Be sure that what you are watching is uplifting, moral, and presents realistic consequences.

The ultimate communication media available to us is the Bible, the inspired Word of God. The Bible has a treasure chest of stories inspired by the Holy Spirit to help us walk out our destinies. The Bible is the complete instruction manual for victorious living, full of vivid illustrations. There are great lessons to be learned by reading and studying the lives of the characters in God's Word. Romans 15:4 says so: "Whatever things were written before were written *for our learning*, that we through the patience and comfort of the Scriptures might have hope."

What an amazing thought! We can learn from the stories in God's Word before we even encounter adverse circumstances. The lives revealed within the pages of the Bible are like fruit in an orchard, waiting to be plucked so they can nourish our souls. Listen to this verse from 2 Timothy 3:16–17: "All Scripture is given by inspiration of God, and is profitable for doctrine, for reproof, for correction, for instruction in righteousness, that the man of God may be complete, thoroughly equipped for every good work."

LEARNING FROM OTHERS' SUCCESSES

There are many advantages to learning from the successes of others. It should become a way of life for you. Take a look at these illustrations:

There's Nobody behind Me

Throughout my medical career, I have had the privilege of working with some great surgeons. The best of these is Carla Hawley-Bowland, MD. She was one of my attending physicians during residency from 1992 to 1996 at William Beaumont Army Medical Center in El Paso. She was a lieutenant colonel and the residency program director my last three years. I was thrilled when she became the first female physician in the history of the army to make the rank of general officer. When I last saw her in October of 2007, she had made two stars or major general, and was commander of Tripler Army Medical Center.

She later became commander of Walter Reed Army Medical Center in Washington, DC. She delivered our youngest daughter, Rebekah, during my first year of training. She still calls me Nate.

There were times during my residency when I had difficult deliveries or surgeries and needed her assistance. She was always able to accomplish with ease what seemed difficult for me. On these occasions, with a satisfied smile, she would often ask, "Nate, you know why I was able to delivery this baby? Because *I'm staff and there's nobody behind* me. If I can't do it, it doesn't happen." Those words have resounded in my mind over the years. They have helped me through many obstetrical or surgical emergencies when lives were on the line. I learned there are times and situations in life where if you don't succeed, the results can be catastrophic. You and you alone are responsible for the success of the mission. Failure is not an option. Thank you, General Hawley-Bowland.

Give Me Two Strong Men

In August of 2002 I was transferred from Tripler to Fort Sill, Oklahoma. I turned in my military house keys at the beginning of the week. Libby and Rebekah flew out to Kentucky to spend some time with her family. I decided to stay five more days in Honolulu with our other daughters, Katherine and Victoria, before reporting to my next duty station. Our local church, Word of Life Christian Center, was celebrating its eighteenth anniversary on Sunday, and I wanted to be present for the services and celebration.

I had attended Bible school at Word of Life for eighteen months and volunteered in various capacities on Sundays. My last year in the church, I served as an usher-greeter. The guest speaker for the Sunday morning and evening services was the pastor of a large church in California. I had always wanted to hear him in person. I invested time, energy, and resources by staying five days in a hotel, with plans to fly to Oklahoma on Monday. I was making an investment to gain knowledge and wisdom. My expectations were high. I did my part. I had a high expectation God was going to do His.

The Sunday morning services were very good. The ushers blessed me by throwing a going-away lunch at the church in my honor. They gave me a beautiful lei made of burgundy fabric. That lei still hangs on the wall by my library desk. So far the day had exceeded my expectations. I could not wait until the Sunday evening service.

I had to run a few errands before the evening service because I was checking out of the hotel in the morning to catch my flight. I arrived at the church shortly after the service had begun. Herb, the head usher, and his brother Bobby both saw me when I came into the sanctuary. The church was packed and the service was in the middle of praise and worship. Herb motioned for me to come up to the first row. He gave me his seat so I could be up close. I still had my lei on from earlier that day. I was having the time of my life. It was only going to get better.

The message was excellent. The minister was speaking on holding fast to the confession of your faith from Hebrews 4:14: "Seeing then that we have a great High Priest who has passed through the heavens, Jesus the Son of God, let us hold fast our confession."

The speaker, at the foot of the stage, was walking back and forth while preaching. He then asked for a large prayer cloth and said, *"Give me two strong men. I don't want any weak men. I want two strong men!"*

When I heard him say that, I immediately bounded out of my chair and started walking toward him. Philippians 4:13 came to mind: "I can do all things through Christ who strengthens me." *If Christ strengthens me, then that makes me a strong man!* I reasoned. Since the minister had asked for a strong man, I was simply obeying his request.

Several other thoughts were racing through my mind as I began walking toward the speaker. I thought about one of my favorite verses, Proverbs 21:22: "A wise man scales the city of the mighty, and brings down the trusted stronghold." I was thinking that if a wise man can bring down a whole city, surely I can bring down one strong man, whoever that might be. There were a handful of powerful men in the congregation I was hoping would not step forward. I might have a harder time winning.

Lastly, I thought, "If I make a fool of myself, I'm leaving on a plane tomorrow anyway. They'll never see me again." By this time I had arrived at center stage with the lei around my neck. I looked like a tourist in need of directions. Two thousand people were looking on, waiting to see what would happen next.

The speaker looked me up and down. He was a comical guy by nature. At six feet and 188 pounds, we all could tell he was unimpressed by my physique. He wasn't hesitant to let me know about it, either! I'll never forget what he said next. "Looks are deceiving; I want you to know that." He was being sarcastic. I smiled and nodded my head in agreement as if to say, "Yes, looks are deceiving." I was really motivated to win after that remark! Bobby the usher, a former U.S. marine, was thinking the same thing I was thinking: "You have no idea who you are talking to." The senior pastor, seated twenty feet away, was trying to suppress a huge grin.

Most of the people in the church of about six thousand knew who I was. They were polite not to laugh at me. The Hawaiian and the Samoan Islands have some of the biggest and strongest men you will find anywhere. I once watched an ESPN special on Samoan athletes. I was amazed to learn that if you are Samoan, you are sixty times more likely to play in the National Football League than somebody from any other part of the world! This is due in part to their size, upper body strength, and agility. One of the pastors on staff at Word of Life, a Samoan, was a former NFL lineman and World's Strongest Man competitor. Our church was full of guys like this. I was dwelling in a land of giants. For me to walk up to the front of that audience as a *strong man* was a joke. Just the same, my dear Hawaiian brothers and sisters didn't laugh at me, but I was thinking they must be really amused.

We only had to wait five seconds for my adversary to step forward.

Down the middle aisle he came. I had never seen him before. He was either new to the church or visiting. He was a light-skinned man, my age, about five foot eleven. He must have weighed 230 pounds and was built like a fullback. His biceps were straining at the sleeves of his polo shirt, and you could see the bulge of his thighs through his slacks. The speaker saw him coming, looked at him and then at me, and said, "There you go," as if to say, "Now look what you have gotten yourself into!" I just smiled back.

Mr. Fullback and I stood facing the audience for several minutes while the speaker continued to preach on faith. He then paused and walked toward the two of us standing nearby. He rolled the three-by-three-foot prayer cloth into a makeshift rope and gave each of us one end. You guessed it. This was going to be a "tug of war." I held my end of the rope with my left hand and wrapped the cloth around my right forearm and gave it a friendly tug. The crowd, and the speaker, both went "oooooh." They were really into it now. There might be somersaults before this was over!

The speaker then explained that my opponent represented the devil, who was trying to take away God's promises in their lives. The rope represented the promises of God. He then tapped my shoulder and said I represented the audience that has to *hold fast* to what they believe God for.

He was gesturing passionately with his arms. "It's about faith and receiving the promises of God!" he exclaimed.

"Yes!" and "Amen!" resounded from the crowd.

My opponent's eyes were following the speaker. I had my eyes fixed on his end of the rope. I only had a split second of opportunity. Once the crowd's excitement reached its peak, the speaker said, "OK. Take it from him, Mr. Devil—"

By the time he said "Mr. Devil" I had already given the rope a little slack. I pulled back on the rope with everything I had at the exact moment he finished his sentence. The rope slipped out of my opponent's hands! In a fraction of a second the contest was over.

The crowd went wild and burst out laughing! There were people crying, holding their sides, slapping their seats. My opponent's face had turned beet red from embarrassment. The speaker was not expecting this. I could tell he was amused, nonetheless. I waved my "prize" above my head, which made everyone laugh even more. The audience applauded in approval. My brother and I went back to our seats and the minister continued the sermon.

How did I defeat my "opponent" in this story? Obviously it was not with brute strength. It was with wisdom and observation knowledge I had learned from the success of others.

Twenty-two years earlier, while in high school, I read a story about a competition between the two toughest men in a crowd. A giant of a man stepped forward. Everyone was afraid of him and nobody wanted to challenge him except for one guy. He was of average height and thin. Everyone looked at the challenger like he was crazy. The giant was looking forward to crushing him, the same way Goliath menaced and growled at David. Like David, the small challenger defeated his Goliath. He beat him with the same strategy that wins many military battles—the element of surprise. That was exactly what I did with my opponent, and he was never able to recover. I beat my giant with knowledge I acquired as a high school sophomore.

The Bible says this: "Wise people store up knowledge, but the mouth of the foolish is near destruction" (Proverbs 10:14). And again it says: "A wise man is strong, yes, a man of knowledge increases strength" (Proverbs 24:5).

You now have two illustrations showing how you can learn from the successes of others through either direct observation or indirect observation using communication media. Now let's look at an illustration of learning from the successes of others using television media, another indirect observation method.

Mind over Matter

Brett Favre, the legendary football player, currently holds the record for the most consecutive NFL starts by a quarterback. He has done this despite playing hurt and while going through personal tragedy. I remember watching him during a television interview. He was asked how he managed to play week after week despite sometimes being in severe physical pain. I'll never forget what he said: "Mind over matter. If you don't mind, it don't matter." That bit of advice has helped me over the years.

You Cannot Lose If...

We all go through challenges in life. It's easy to say, "I give up." We have an opportunity every day to give up on the things God has called us to do. It's easy to quit on your dreams and settle for less, but there is no joy or victory in quitting. There were so many times in my life I could have quit.

I could have quit when I lived in Guatemala by myself in a room the size of a jail cell. I could have quit when my father died seven months later. I could have quit when I came to the United States and lived in eight different home environments during high school. I could have quit when I went to college to try to get ahead. I could have quit when I went straight from three months of infantry officer basic training on Friday and started medical school on Monday with no time to rest. I could have quit when I started medical school not even knowing where my classroom was, living in an empty apartment. I could have quit when I worked 85 to 105 hours a week during residency, with three children and Libby finishing her PhD. I could have quit when God told me to go to Bible school and I had to rearrange my work schedule for eighteen months. I could have quit when I was working at times ninety hours a week and studying to write this book. I could have quit on coming to Tulsa after six years of standing in faith to do so while serving in the military. I could have quit on writing this book because it was unfamiliar territory.

If I had quit just one day during these seasons in my life, you would not be reading this book today. I want to encourage you. *Don't quit!* The rewards are eternal. Tap into God's grace, or supernatural ability.

These are some of the affirmations that helped me get through some pretty tough times. I also want to share with you some of my favorite scriptures on overcoming, and a word the Lord gave me to help me through the most difficult storms.

1. *No Excuses/No Quitting.* No matter where I am in life or what I am going through, I will not make excuses for myself. I will not use past or present circumstances as

excuses for not pursuing God's promises in my life. No matter how difficult or how long it takes to do what God has called me to do, I will not quit! "Brethren, I do not count myself to have apprehended; but one thing I do, forgetting those things which are behind and reaching forward to those things which are ahead, I press toward the goal for the prize of the upward call of God in Christ Jesus" (Philippians 3:13–14).

2. *I will not let go of my dream.* I may be hanging from a cliff by a rope, but that rope is tied around my arm in a knot. I am not going anywhere. I might as well enjoy the scenery while I'm up here. Time and pain are irrelevant. It may take me awhile to climb up on that ledge, but with God's help I will do it. No matter what happens, I will not let go of my dream! "I can do all things through Christ who strengthens me" (Philippians 4:13).

3. *Raise your faith threshold.* I will not wait for my faith to be tested. I will put my faith to the test now. Faith is like a muscle. It must be exercised and developed. "My brethren, count it all joy when you fall into various trials, knowing that the testing of your faith produces patience. But let patience have its perfect work, that you may be perfect and complete, lacking nothing" (James 1:2–4).

The Lord gave me a word one day when I was going through a very difficult time. I have never forgotten it. This is not a quote from the Bible, it is a message God impressed on my mind and heart.

"When Peter got out of the boat, he did so because he was motivated by love. Faith works by love. And when he began to sink he still had his eyes on Me. That is hope. There is love, there is faith, and there is hope. But the greatest of these is love. And when he cried out to Me, I immediately reached down with My righteous right hand and lifted him up. That is the power of My grace. You cannot lose if you keep your eyes on Me. You cannot lose if you keep your eyes on Me. I AM the author and the finisher of your faith."

Jesus is the author and finisher of our faith. As long as we keep our eyes on Him, everything is going to work out. "Looking unto Jesus, the author and finisher of our faith, who for the joy that was set before Him endured the cross, despising the shame, and has sat down at the right hand of the throne of God" (Hebrews 12:2).

LEARNING FROM OTHERS' MISTAKES

Learning from others' mistakes can be just as profitable as learning from their successes—but it takes humility. The following Bible story illustrates this point perfectly.

Elijah and the Three Captains

The first chapter of 2 Kings tells the story of King Ahaziah and Elijah the prophet. Ahaziah injured himself one day and sent messengers to inquire of the false god Baal-Zebub whether he would recover. The angel of the Lord informed Elijah of the king's doing and sent the prophet to intercept his messengers. Elijah confronted the messengers of the king for not consulting the one true God. The prophet instructed the king's envoys to tell their master he was going to die. The king was angry when he heard the report from Elijah and sent his men to find Elijah and bring him in. In 2 Kings 1:9–10 we read:

> *The king sent to him a captain of fifty with his fifty men. So he went up to him; and there he was, sitting on the top of a hill. And he spoke to him: "Man of God, the king has said, 'Come down!'" So Elijah answered and said to the captain of fifty, "If I am a man of God, then let fire come down from heaven and consume you and your fifty men." And fire came down from heaven and consumed him and his fifty.*

The first captain of fifty made a deadly mistake. He treated Elijah the prophet with contempt and it cost him and all fifty of his men their lives. Let's read 2 Kings 1:11 and find out what happened next: "Then he [the king] sent to him [Elijah] another captain of fifty with his fifty men. And he answered and said to him: "'Man of God, thus has the king said, "Come down quickly!"'"

The second captain was proud and did not learn from the first captain's mistake. He was more insolent to Elijah than the first commander. He told Elijah to come down *quickly*, as if to say *right now* or *move it*. Proverbs 16:18 says pride goes before destruction, and that's exactly what happened to the second captain. Let's read from 2 Kings 1:12: "Elijah answered and said to them, 'If I am a man of God, let fire come down from heaven and consume you and your fifty men' And the fire of God came down from heaven and consumed him and his fifty."

I guess you could say that things had really heated up at this point! A frustrated King Ahaziah then sent a *third* captain with fifty men to take Elijah. The third captain, however, learned from the two men who had gone before him. He humbled himself and learned from their fatal mistakes. He approached Elijah, the man of God, with reverential respect as recorded in 2 Kings 1:13–14:

> *The third captain of fifty went up, and came and fell on his knees before Elijah, and pleaded with him, and said to him: "Man of God, please let my life and the life of these fifty servants of yours be precious in your sight. Look, fire has come down from heaven and burned up the first two captains of fifties with their fifties. But let my life now be precious in your sight."*

What a story! The third captain, having learned from the mistakes of the first two captains, was rewarded for his humility. Notice God's response to the third captain's act of humility in 2 Kings 1:15: "The angel of the LORD said to Elijah, 'Go down with him; do not be afraid of him.' So he arose and went down with him to the king."

We have covered the second step in making a wise decision: learning from others' successes and mistakes. There are seven questions you have to ask yourself when making a wise decision. These are the questions we have addressed in Step #1 and Step #2:

Question #1—What have I learned from personal successes and mistakes?

Question #2:—What have I learned from others' successes and mistakes?

Once you have answered questions 1 and 2, you are ready to move on to the second level of knowledge and Step #3 in making a wise decision.

DISCUSSION

1. What is the second category of knowledge for operating in wisdom?

2. Give some examples of where you have learned and benefited from others' successes.

3. Give some examples of where you have learned and benefited from others' mistakes.

4. Give some examples of where you failed to learn from others' successes or mistakes and paid the price. Did you learn your lesson the first time around? Why or why not?

5. What are some of the rewards for learning from others' successes and mistakes?

6. What kind of practical things can you do to grow in the second category of knowledge?

7. What is the second question you have to ask yourself in making a wise decision?

CHAPTER 8

The Second Level of Knowledge: Education

The ear that hears the rebukes of life will abide
among the wise. He who disdains instruction
despises his own soul, but he who heeds rebuke
gets understanding. The fear of the LORD *is*
the instruction of wisdom, and before honor is
humility.—Proverbs 15:31–33

Proverbs 15:31–33 is the foundational passage for this teaching on decision making. Each verse makes reference to one of the three levels of knowledge. Verse 32 speaks about the second level of knowledge, that is, education knowledge. "He who disdains *instruction* despises his own soul, but he who heeds *rebuke* gets understanding."

Webster's College Dictionary defines education as a *process* of one kind or another:

1a: the action or *process* of educating or of being educated

1b: the knowledge and development resulting from an educational *process*

A synonym for the word education is the word *training*. Education and training both refer to the *process* of being taught. Education is the general term for institutional learning and implies the guidance and training intended to develop a person's full capabilities and intelligence; for example, a high school education. Training suggests exercise or practice to gain skill, endurance, or facility in a specific field; for example, training in self-defense.

Education knowledge is knowledge gained through a process of teaching or instruction from others. Education knowledge is broken down into the third and fourth categories of knowledge or learning:

Category #3: learning from technical knowledge (education and training above)

Category #4: learning from wise counsel (godly advice for solving life problems)

Education knowledge, unlike observation knowledge, requires a *greater* investment of time, energy, and resources. Humility will enable you to gain education knowledge, while pride will prevent you from doing so. As you grow in knowledge, you will need more humility and have to deal more with pride. The reason for this is that knowledge puffs up. (See 1 Corinthians 8:1.) Do you remember the Twelve Rules of Knowledge we discussed in chapter 6? Rules 9 and 10 deal with humility and pride, respectively.

9, Humility, like strength, enables you to climb the mountain of knowledge. In the parable of the king and the valley, Samuel represents humility.

10. Pride, like gravity, resists you from climbing the mountain of knowledge. In the parable of the king and the valley, Eliab represents pride.

The Line of Demarcation

In chapter 6 we discussed the Twelve Rules of Knowledge. Rule number 5 says the following: Non-Christians can only operate in the three lowest categories of knowledge, while Christians have the capability of operating in all six categories.

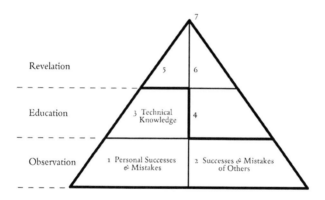

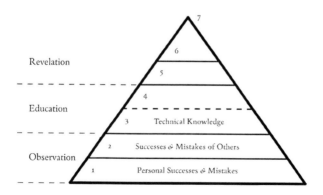

There is a line of demarcation between the third and fourth categories of knowledge. This is similar to the tree line on a mountain. Trees can go no farther after you reach a certain elevation on a mountain. There is a line of demarcation, or tree line, between categories of knowledge 3 and 4. Categories 1 to 3 deal with *natural* knowledge, while categories 4 to 6 deal with *spiritual* knowledge. People who are not born again and filled with the Spirit of God can only operate in natural knowledge. People who are born again through faith in Jesus Christ, and filled with the Spirit of God, are capable of operating in natural and spiritual knowledge. As it says in 1 Corinthians 2:14: "The natural man does not receive the things of the Spirit of God, for they are foolishness to him; nor can he know them, because they are spiritually discerned." Though this says "man," the reference is to "mankind" and indicates both man and woman.

The *natural man* is the man who is not born again. Though physically alive, he is spiritually dead and unable to discern spiritual knowledge. The *spiritual man* is the man who is born again. He is physically alive but also spiritually alive. He is able to discern spiritual knowledge.

There is actually a third category, that of the *carnal man*. This is the man who is born again, a new creation in Christ, but his mind is not renewed to the Word of God. Another term for this is baby Christian. This is someone who is led by the flesh rather than the Spirit of God. You can be born again twenty years and be more of a baby Christian than someone who has been walking with Christ for six months. So this is a term based on spiritual maturity rather than physical age. Romans 8:6–7 says: "To be *carnally* minded is death, but to be spiritually minded is life and peace. Because the *carnal* mind is enmity against God; for it is not subject to the law of God, nor indeed can be."

The carnal man, although born again, is not able to operate in spiritual knowledge until his mind is renewed by God's Word. Notice Paul is speaking to Christians in Romans 12:1–2: "I beseech you therefore, brethren, by the mercies of God, that you present your bodies a living sacrifice, holy, acceptable to God, which is your reasonable service. And do not be conformed to this world, but be transformed by the *renewing* of your mind, that you may prove what is that good and acceptable and perfect will of God."

You cannot underestimate the importance of education knowledge. Growing and maturing to this level of knowledge is key to your success. You must make increasing in technical knowledge and wise counsel a way of life. "A wise man will hear and increase *learning,* and a man of understanding will attain *wise counsel,* to understand a proverb and an enigma, the words of the wise and their riddles" (Proverbs 1:5–6).

Remember that wisdom is a range of acquired knowledge rightly applied. You have to invest of your time, energy, and resources to gain education knowledge. "The heart of the prudent *acquires* knowledge, and the ear of the wise *seeks* knowledge" (Proverbs 18:15).

God can and does use anyone He chooses. But those He uses most have two things in common: consecration and preparation. Another good word for preparation is education. I'm not referring to a diploma, but rather a consecrated vessel who has gone through a process of educational growth fit for the Master's use.

The Bible gives us many examples of people who have done this. Moses was one of them. God supernaturally made a way for Moses to be raised and educated by Pharaoh's daughter. Acts 7:22 says: "Moses was *learned* in all the wisdom of the Egyptians, and was mighty in words and deeds."

Daniel was taken captive to Babylon, along with three of his friends, Hananiah, Mishael, and Azariah. You might recognize them more easily by their Babylonian names of Shadrach, Meshach, and Abednego. God opened a door of opportunity for them to receive a Babylonian education to complement their knowledge of God and His Word. Their educations made them highly effective and greatly increased their sphere of influence so that God could strategically use them. Daniel 1:17–19 says:

> *As for these four young men, God gave them knowledge and skill in all literature and wisdom; and Daniel had understanding in all visions and dreams. Now at the end of the days, when the king had said that they should be brought in, the chief of the eunuchs brought them in before Nebuchadnezzar. Then the king interviewed them, and among them all none was found like Daniel, Hananiah, Mishael, and Azariah; therefore they served before the king.*

It does not matter what educational or technical background you have. God can use you in any sphere of influence. But my medical background as an obstetrician and gynecological surgeon has enabled me to touch people's lives in a way that few people can. I am thankful for the honor and privilege of patient care. Having said that, I am continually growing in knowledge in different areas of life. I have attended two different Bible schools. I am constantly reading books, listening to educational CDs, watching informative television programs, and attending conferences. I desire to grow as a person in order to connect with and reach my world for the Lord. I want to encourage you to do the same. Strive to grow as a person and see how God can use you.

You have now been introduced to the second level of knowledge, which is education knowledge. You now know the two categories of education knowledge: technical knowledge and wise counsel. Technical knowledge and wise counsel represent the third and fourth categories of knowledge overall. You have been warned about the role of humility and pride when it comes to education knowledge. And you also know about the line of demarcation that exists between categories 3 and 4 of knowledge.

Once you have mastered Step #1 and Step #2 in the first level of knowledge, you are ready to move on to Step #3 and Step #4 in the second level of knowledge. It would be wise to review the Twelve Rules of Knowledge at the end of chapter 6 before you move on. Let's review rules 4 and 12, respectively, before you continue.

4. Each level and category of knowledge builds on the preceding level and category.

12. There are seven steps in making a wise decision that is based on knowledge.

Discussion

1. What is the second level of knowledge?

2. What are the two categories in education knowledge?

3. How does education knowledge differ from observation knowledge?

4. Education knowledge requires a greater investment of _____, _____, and _____.

5. Where does the line of demarcation between natural knowledge and spiritual knowledge take place?

6. Explain the difference between the natural, spiritual, and carnal man.

7. Why can the spiritual man operate in natural and spiritual knowledge?

8. Is it possible for a carnal Christian to operate in spiritual knowledge? Explain.

9. Give some examples of decisions you made as a natural, spiritual, or carnal man.

10. Would you agree that it pays to be spiritually minded? Why?

STEP #3: LEARNING FROM TECHNICAL KNOWLEDGE

He who disdains instruction despises his own soul, but he who heeds rebuke gets understanding.—Proverbs 15:32

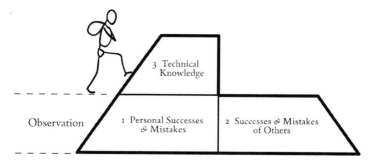

We have seen that education is knowledge gained through a process of teaching or instruction from others. Education knowledge is broken down into the third and fourth categories of knowledge or learning:

Category #3: learning from technical knowledge (education and training)

Category #4: learning from wise counsel (godly advice for solving life problems)

In this chapter we will learn about category #3, or technical knowledge.

WHAT IS TECHNICAL KNOWLEDGE?

Let's review for a moment:

We have learned that technical knowledge means essentially two things: *education* and *training*. *Education* is the general term for institutional learning and implies the guidance and training intended to develop a person's full capabilities and intelligence, such as a high school education. *Training* suggests exercise or practice to gain skill, endurance, or facility in a specific field, such as training in self-defense. It may help you to think of *education* as classroom learning and *training* as hands-on learning. Both are important.

In order to become a physician, I needed both education and training. I had to go through four years of college and two years of medical school before I ever saw a patient as a third-year medical student. As I completed medical school and residency, I grew in medical knowledge and practical skills as an obstetrician-gynecologist. I have been practicing independently since I completed my residency in 1996. I still continue to grow, however, in both medical knowledge and hands-on skills. This is one of the things I enjoy about what I do. You never stop learning. Wisdom is a lifestyle of learning. "Listen to counsel and receive *instruction*, that you may be wise in your latter days" (Proverbs 19:20).

TECHNICAL KNOWLEDGE IN DAILY LIVING, ETHICAL, AND GOAL-ORIENTED DECISIONS

In chapter 3 we read about the three types of decisions: daily living, ethical, and goal-oriented. Technical knowledge is distinct from the other five categories of knowledge for one reason. Technical knowledge is useful for daily living and goal-oriented decisions, but not for ethical decisions. The reason is that ethical decisions are not based on technical knowledge. Ethical decisions are based on right and wrong with the Bible as the standard. Having the technical capability to do something doesn't make it right. You must always go back to the Word of God. The Ten Commandments in Exodus 20 are a good place to start.

Daily living Decisions

Technical knowledge is important in our daily lives because we live in a modern, technological society. We need technical knowledge for everything from using the TV remote to driving a car. The more technical knowledge you have, the more you can get accomplished. For example, before e-mail and mail groups existed, it was necessary to write or call people individually to deliver a message. The same task can now be accomplished in a fraction of the time day or night by using the Internet.

Have You Heard the Weather Report?

When I was a teenager, I wondered why the local news networks devoted so much time to the weather forecast. Now that I drive a car and travel I understand that it's good to know what the weather conditions are outside. I am prepared when we are going to have snow and ice. I keep gloves, ice scraper, and de-icer spray in my car. I keep my cell phone charged up and there's a blanket in the trunk of my car just in case I get delayed somewhere. I have learned these practices from the first and second categories of knowledge, personal and others' successes and mistakes. I use the technical knowledge provided by the weather forecast, along with what I have learned from categories 1 and 2, to get me safely to my destination. Remember rule number

4 of the Twelve Rules of Knowledge: each level and category of knowledge builds on the preceding level and category.

You may be wondering if that's really faith. It isn't. It's wisdom. Faith and wisdom work together. By faith you see your destination and by wisdom you arrive at your destination safely. You do not make decisions based on fear. Wisdom and fear are not compatible. You make decisions based on knowledge. Do you remember the definition of wisdom? It is a range of *acquired knowledge* that is rightly applied. Lastly, make sure you are operating in humility and not pride. You don't want to be like the guy in the dented blue sedan racing down an icy road that we talked about earlier. That is neither faith nor wisdom. That, my friend, is pride and foolishness. Let's read Proverbs 14:12: "There is a way that seems right to a man, but its end is the way of death."

What you hear next may challenge your thinking, but it should also bring you clarity.

Make Decisions Based on Knowledge, Not Faith

Let me say it again. *You make decisions based on knowledge, not faith.* Please do not misunderstand. I am not saying faith is not important. Faith is very important. Remember I told you earlier that faith and wisdom work together. You need both.

I used the analogy of you standing at the foot of a mountain you wish to climb. By faith you saw yourself standing on the peak. By wisdom you made good decisions about how you would reach the peak. Wise decisions require knowledge. This is where some people miss it. They try to use their faith to get results when in actuality they need more wisdom, or *a range of acquired knowledge rightly applied*. When you combine your faith with godly wisdom things really begin to happen.

Knowledge Precedes Wisdom and Faith

Wisdom and faith require knowledge. "The heart of the prudent *acquires* knowledge, and the ear of the wise *seeks* knowledge" (Proverbs 18:15). "So then *faith* comes by hearing, and hearing by the word of God" (Romans 10:17).

The common denominator between wisdom and faith is revelation knowledge of God's Word. Wisdom requires a range of acquired knowledge as well as revelation knowledge of God's Word by the Holy Spirit. Godly faith requires revelation knowledge about God's Word exclusively. The greater your knowledge, and belief, in God's Word, the greater will be your faith. Knowledge precedes faith. You can have knowledge without faith in God's Word. The children of Israel knew the Word of God to go in and possess the land, but they failed to mix the Word of God with faith. Hebrews 4:2 says: "The word which they heard did not profit them, not being mixed with faith in those who heard it."

The children of Israel received the negative report of the ten spies and died in the wilderness with them. But Joshua and Caleb knew God's Word and mixed it with faith. They led the next generation of Israel into the promised land to possess it.

Some people who do not understand the biblical decision-making process may think all you need is knowledge. But intellect is not enough. You want to avoid what I call the *knowledge pitfall.* The Bible tells us in 1 Corinthians 8:1 that knowledge puffs up. Knowledge alone will not get you God results. God will see to it that you have to exercise faith in Him and His Word at some point. The Bible tells us to examine and test ourselves as to whether we are in the faith. "Examine yourselves as to whether you are in the faith. Test yourselves" (2 Corinthians 13:5).

I believe you can look at this passage of scripture a couple of different ways. First, we are to examine ourselves to see if we are really living the Christian life. Second, we are to examine ourselves to see if we are really operating in faith. As you can see from the story of Joshua and Caleb, it's necessary to mix knowledge with faith. Wisdom and faith work together.

This next question might be hard to swallow.

Are You a Person of Wisdom or Faith?

What would you say if you were asked this question? If you had to choose between being a person of wisdom and a person of faith, which would it be? Before you answer, consider what you've learned about how wisdom and faith are similar and how they are different.

If you answered, "I would rather be a person of wisdom," you answered correctly. The reason for this is that faith falls within the realm of wisdom and not the other way around. Are you shaking your head and asking how this could be? Let me explain it another way. *A person of wisdom will always have faith, but a person of faith will not always be wise.*

The reason the above statement is true is that a person of wisdom operates in all three levels of knowledge, whereas a person of faith operates in revelation knowledge only. A person of wisdom, like Solomon, may not always make the best decisions, but at least he knows how. The biblical decision-making process shows you how to make good decisions. But whether you do or not is entirely up to you. God will not override your will.

Daniel and Samson are good examples. Both are listed among the heroes of faith in Hebrews chapter 11.

Daniel rose from the ashes of Babylonian captivity to trusted administrator for four kings. Samson, through foolish disobedience, lost his eyes and was imprisoned by the Philistines. These two men had different fates primarily because Daniel was a person of wisdom and faith and Samson was a person of faith but lacked wisdom. A person of wisdom has both the faith and the know-how to achieve a thing. Not all people of faith have the know-how or wisdom to make the right choices. This is why Solomon so accurately said that wisdom is the principal thing in Proverbs 4:7–9: "Wisdom is the principal thing; therefore get wisdom. And in all your getting, get understanding. Exalt her, and she will promote you; she will bring you honor, when you embrace her. She will place on your head an ornament of grace; a crown of glory she will deliver to you."

Wisdom Is the Principal Thing

Wisdom encompasses not only faith, but so much more. At the beginning of the book of Proverbs, in chapter 1, verses 1–7, Solomon gives a discourse on the attributes of wisdom.

The proverbs of Solomon the son of David, king of Israel: to know wisdom and instruction, to perceive the words of understanding, to receive the instruction of wisdom, justice, judgment, and equity; to give prudence to the simple, to the young man knowledge and discretion—a wise man will hear and increase learning, and a man of understanding will attain wise counsel, to understand a proverb and an enigma, the words of the wise and their riddles. The fear of the LORD *is the beginning of knowledge, but fools despise wisdom and instruction.*

Wisdom encompasses knowing, perceiving, receiving instruction, prudence, discretion, hearing, understanding, and fear of the Lord. We stated earlier that the fear of the Lord means reverential respect for God.

Wisdom also encompasses God-given talents or abilities. Huram from Tyre was a man gifted in working with bronze. He helped Solomon with the construction of the temple in Jerusalem. "King Solomon sent and brought Huram from Tyre. . . a bronze worker; he was filled with *wisdom* and understanding and skill in working with all kinds of bronze work. So he came to King Solomon and did all his work" (1 Kings 7:13–14).

Wisdom also encompasses revelation knowledge from the Holy Spirit. The Holy Spirit is called the Spirit of Wisdom. "I also, after I heard of your faith in the Lord Jesus and your love for all the saints, do not cease to give thanks for you, making mention of you in my prayers: that the God of our Lord Jesus Christ, the Father of glory, may give to you the *spirit of wisdom and revelation* in the knowledge of Him" (Ephesians 1:15–17).

The prophet Isaiah spoke about the coming of Jesus, the Messiah, centuries before He appeared on earth. He prophesied that the Holy Spirit or Spirit of Wisdom would rest upon Him. "There shall come forth a Rod from the stem of Jesse, and a Branch shall grow out of his roots. The Spirit of the LORD shall rest upon Him, the *Spirit of wisdom* and understanding, the Spirit of counsel and might, the Spirit of knowledge and of the fear of the LORD" (Isaiah 11:1–2).

Wisdom also encompasses spiritual gifts, as we read in 1 Corinthians 12:4, 7–11:

> *There are diversities of gifts, but the same Spirit. But the manifestation of the Spirit is given to each one for the profit of all: for to one is given the word of wisdom through the Spirit, to another the word of knowledge through the same Spirit, to another faith by the same Spirit, to another gifts of healings by the same Spirit, to another the working of miracles, to another prophecy, to another discerning of spirits, to another different kinds of tongues, to another the interpretation of tongues. But one and the same Spirit works all these things, distributing to each one individually as He wills.*

We will talk more about spiritual gifts later. As you can see from the previous scriptures, wisdom encompasses many attributes of God's divine nature.

Wisdom

Anointing	Discretion
Fear of the Lord	Faith
Fruit of the Spirit	God-given Talents
Hearing	Knowing
Perceiving	Prudence
Receiving Instruction	Revelation Knowledge
Spiritual Gifts	Understanding

The need for wisdom is particularly evident in the area of goal-oriented decisions. Technical knowledge is essential in achieving personal and God given-goals.

Do You Mind If I Watch?

It doesn't matter if it's the plumber, shower-door installer, garbage-disposal man, heating and cooling technician, refrigerator-maintenance guy, oven expert, floor-tile worker, painter, sprinkler repairman, lawn professional, or fence builder. They have all been to my house and looked a little surprised when I asked, "Do you mind if I watch while you're working?"

So far the response has been positive. They think it's great that a doctor is interested in what they are doing. They're glad to share their technical knowledge, and I'm glad to invest time, energy, and resources to learn from them. Sometimes they will ask me medical questions and I have an opportunity to be a blessing to them. I had the privilege of leading one of them back to the Lord.

Knowledge has its rewards. It pays to ask questions when you run into someone who knows more than you do. Proverbs

15:14 says: "The heart of him who has understanding seeks knowledge."

GOAL-ORIENTED DECISIONS

Technical knowledge is of the utmost importance when making quality goal-oriented decisions. The bigger the decision you're making, the greater the amount of technical knowledge you will need. You buy wisdom by investing of your time, energy, and resources. "Buy the truth, and do not sell it, also wisdom and instruction and understanding" (Proverbs 23:23). Rules of knowledge 8 and 11 from the Twelve Rules of Knowledge say the following:

8. The higher the level of knowledge you desire, the more time, energy, and resources you will have to invest to acquire it.

11. The greater the amount of knowledge you have acquired, the easier and more beneficial a decision becomes.

You should see acquiring knowledge as an investment rather than an expense.

HOW DO I GET OUT OF THIS PARKING LOT?

Over a three-year period, our local church, Victory Christian Center, completed construction of a five-thousand-seat worship center debt-free.

I got to thinking, though, that more seats inside mean more cars in the parking lot. Once the building was completed, how would we handle more traffic with the current number of entrances and exits into the facility?

Then one Sunday we were told that traffic engineers had been consulted on how to maximize flow of vehicles in and out of the property. An extra lane here, a couple of bridges over there and problem solved. Time, energy, and resources were invested to acquire the necessary technical knowledge. The results were outstanding. It is easy to enter and exit any service at the church. "Through wisdom a house is built, and by understanding it is established" (Proverbs 24:3).

You Do Not Have a Problem

If you are trying to make goal-oriented decisions and don't know what to do, remember this: *You don't have a problem. You need more knowledge.*

There is no problem wisdom can't solve. Just because you don't have the answer doesn't mean there is no answer. If you really want the answer, though, you are going to have to invest time, energy, and resources to acquire the necessary knowledge. How much are you willing to invest?

I took a week of vacation time to attend Victory's Word Explosion Conference in August of 2006. That cost me something. I invested time, energy, and resources because I needed knowledge on how to write this book. The Lord gave me the outline for the book, but I needed a format. My search for wisdom was rewarded. One of the speakers shared how he wrote his most recent work. When I heard what he had to say, I knew he had handed me the solution I was seeking. The Lord said to me,

"That's it. That's what you're supposed to do." Mission accomplished. During this process I have never felt I had a problem. I just needed more knowledge. If you seek wisdom, you will find it. Proverbs 8:17 says: "I love those who love me, and those who seek me diligently will find me."

You may be thinking, "I understand that I'm supposed to invest time, energy, and resources to acquire the knowledge I need. But how am I supposed to know where to go for that knowledge?" That's a good question, and I have a great answer—the Holy Spirit! John 14:16–17 says: "I will pray the Father, and He will give you another Helper, that He may abide with you forever—the Spirit of truth, whom the world cannot receive, because it neither sees Him nor knows Him; but you know Him, for He dwells with you and will be with you."

God wants you to gain the wisdom you need more than you do. He wants you to succeed. He has given you, as a Christian, the Holy Spirit to help you every step of the way. Your job is to be sensitive to His voice and cooperate with Him. You can acquire the wisdom you need for any situation if you are willing to cooperate with the Holy Spirit and invest the necessary time, energy, and resources.

CHANGE YOUR VOCABULARY

I would like to ask you to consider changing the word *problem* in your vocabulary to the word *challenge* or *situation*. Here are a few definitions for problem, challenge, and situation from *Webster's College Dictionary:*

- *Problem*: an intricate unsettled question, a source of perplexity or vexation

- *Challenge*: a stimulating task

- *Situation*:   position with respect to conditions and circumstances

Doesn't *stimulating task* sound better than *a source of perplexity and vexation*? I also like the definition of *situation*, because conditions and circumstances are subject to change if you have wisdom. God does not want you perplexed. He wants you to be a person who overcomes challenges through wisdom. You will be able to help yourself and others. The more you overcome, the more you will grow in confidence, wisdom, and character. As you grow in these areas God can trust you with more, much more. "Whoever keeps the fig tree will eat its fruit; so he who waits on his master will be honored" (Proverbs 27:18).

God can use people who know how to make wise decisions. If you become a Joseph, Moses, Mordecai, or Daniel, He will make sure you get from point A to point B at the right time.

Promised Land–Sized Investment

The children of Israel spent almost four hundred years serving as slaves in Egypt before God raised up Moses to help lead His people out of captivity. The Lord supernaturally effected their release by a demonstration of His power through a series of plagues. God was taking His people to the promised land, flowing with milk and honey (the symbol of abundance). Possessing the land they were promised, however, would require a great deal of military intelligence. They were in the process of making many God-given, goal-oriented decisions and in need of technical knowledge. Where would they get it?

Fortunately, God had a plan. Numbers 13:1–2 tells us: "The LORD spoke to Moses, saying, 'Send men to spy out the land of Canaan, which I am giving to the children of Israel; from each tribe of their fathers you shall send a man, every one a leader among them.'"

God gave Moses specific instructions for spying out the promised land they were to possess. Twelve men, a leader from each tribe, were to go and gather technical knowledge, or information. You notice God did not send Israel blindly into Canaan to possess the promised land. Nor did He automatically tell them everything they needed to know. He wanted them to learn something during the process. God spoke to the children of Israel and instructed them on how to acquire the necessary technical knowledge. They in turn invested time, energy, and resources to gain the technical knowledge needed for a successful military campaign.

We are to cooperate with God in the same way. He shows us how to get the knowledge and then we go after it. Technical knowledge is part of God's plan for you to be successful in your life assignments. It is a partnership between the Lord and His people. Let's read Numbers 13:17–20:

Moses sent them to spy out the land of Canaan, and said to them, "Go up this way into the South, and go up to the mountains, and see what the land is like: whether the people who dwell in it are strong or weak, few or many; whether the land they dwell in

*is good or bad; whether the cities they inhabit are like camps or
strongholds; whether the land is rich or poor; and whether there
are forests there or not."*

The twelve spies set out to acquire an enormous amount of
technical knowledge about Canaan's military strength, popula-
tion, agriculture, cities, fortifications, and natural resources. The
amount of time invested to obtain this knowledge was significant. "They returned from spying out the land after forty days"
(Numbers 13:25).

You may know what happened to the twelve spies from
Numbers 14. Ten of the spies returned with a negative report,
saying the challenge was too great and the inhabitants too fierce.
They urged Moses to ditch the plan. This bad report permeated
the entire camp. God had promised the land to the children of
Israel. They had seen His great miracles in Egypt, as well as in
the wilderness, and yet they did not believe. Unbelievably, the
people wanted to return to slavery in Egypt. They were essentially calling God a weakling and a liar! Moses and Aaron were
on their faces praying to God because of the people's great sin.

Only Caleb and Joshua, from among the twelve spies,
declared they should go up at once and take the land God had
promised. The children of Israel were ready to stone them for
their words. Then the Lord spoke to Moses and Aaron. We read
in Numbers 14:28–31, 33–34:

*"As I live," says the LORD, "just as you have spoken in My hear-
ing, so I will do to you: The carcasses of you who have complained
against Me shall fall in the wilderness . . . from twenty years old*

and above. Except for Caleb the son of Jephunneh and Joshua the son of Nun, you shall by no means enter the land. . . . But your little ones, whom you said would be victims, I will bring in, and they shall know the land which you have despised. And your sons shall be shepherds in the wilderness forty years, and bear the brunt of your infidelity. . . .According to the number of days in which you spied out the land, forty days, for each day you shall bear your guilt one year, namely forty years."

The Bible says that the ten men who brought back the evil report, to make the congregation complain, died by the plague before the LORD. Hebrews 3:19 says: "So we see that they could not enter in *because of unbelief.*" And Hebrews 4:2 says: "But the word which they heard did not profit them, *not being mixed with faith* in those who heard it."

I used this story to point out several things. God had a great promise for the children of Israel. They were about to take on a major goal—possessing the land God had promised them. They needed an enormous amount of technical knowledge to make goal-oriented decisions concerning this great challenge. They invested significant time, energy, and resources to acquire the knowledge needed for decisions in their upcoming military campaign. However, except for Caleb and Joshua, the children of Israel did not mix God's Word with faith. They had the technical knowledge to conquer the land. They had God's promise and backing to conquer the land. They did not, however, have the faith to conquer the land.

Faith and wisdom work together. The children of Israel in this situation had the necessary technical knowledge to possess the land. Knowledge alone, however, does not equal wisdom. Wisdom is *a range of acquired knowledge that is rightly applied.* The children of Israel lacked faith *and* wisdom, which caused them to make a poor decision.

People do not make poor decisions because of a lack of knowledge, anointing, or good intentions. People make poor decisions because of a faulty decision-making process.

In this chapter we have covered the third step in making a wise decision: learning from technical knowledge. There are seven questions you have to ask yourself when making a wise decision.

Question #1—What have I learned from personal successes and mistakes?

Question #2—What have I learned from others' successes and mistakes?

Question #3—What have I learned from technical knowledge?

Once you have answered questions #1 through #3, you will be ready to move on to Step #4 in making a wise decision.

DISCUSSION

1. What is the second level of knowledge?

2. What is the third category of knowledge?

3. Technical knowledge can be broken down to education and instruction. What is the basic difference between the two?

4. What kind of decisions require the most technical knowledge: daily living, ethical, or goal-oriented? Explain.

5. In this chapter we discussed the technical knowledge gained by the twelve spies in the land of Canaan. Can you give some other examples of acquired technical knowledge in the Bible for purposes of goal-oriented decisions?

6. Give examples of technical knowledge you have acquired to help you be successful in some of your daily living and goal-oriented decisions.

7. Give some examples of what has happened to you when you lacked the necessary technical knowledge to make an effective goal-oriented decision.

8. In order to grow in technical knowledge you have to invest of your ____, _____, and _____.

9. Based on our discussion so far, what are the first three questions you have to ask yourself in making a wise decision?

STEP #4: LEARNING FROM WISE COUNSEL

He who disdains instruction despises his own soul, but he who heeds rebuke gets understanding.—Proverbs 15:32

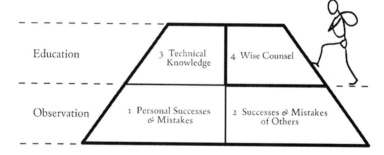

Webster's College Dictionary defines *counsel* as "advice given especially as a result of consultation." The word *advice* means "recommendation regarding a decision or course of conduct: counsel." The Hebrew verb for counsel is *ya`as* (Strong's 3289) and means essentially the same as Webster's definition of counsel above. A simple and useful definition of wise counsel is "godly advice for solving life problems." Wise counsel is essential for making daily living, ethical, and goal-oriented decisions.

The Bible says this: "A wise man will hear and increase learning, and a man of understanding will attain *wise counsel*" (Proverbs 1:5).

The Line of Demarcation

Rule number 5 of the Twelve Rules of Knowledge says this:

5. Non-Christians can only operate in the three lowest categories of knowledge, while Christians have the capability to operate in all six categories.

This line of demarcation or barrier exists between the third and fourth categories of knowledge. The first three categories deal with *natural* knowledge, while categories 4 to 6 deal with *spiritual* knowledge. People who are not born again and filled with the Spirit of God can only operate in natural knowledge. "The *natural* man does not receive the things of the Spirit of God, for they are foolishness to him; nor can he know them, because they are *spiritually* discerned" (1 Corinthians 2:14).

Based on this understanding, there are two primary reasons Christians fail to accept wise council:

1. An unrenewed mind

2. Pride

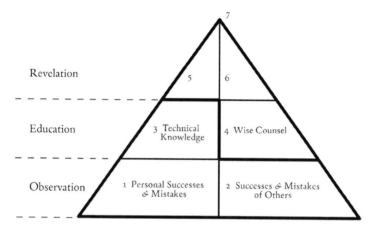

The following graph explains this in a slightly different way.

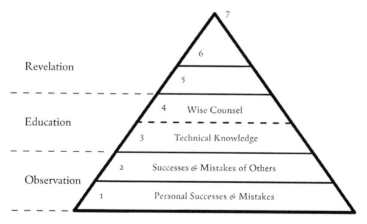

The Unrenewed Mind

The first thing that can cause a Christian to reject wise counsel is an unrenewed mind. Those who are born again through faith in Jesus Christ and filled with the Spirit of God are capable of operating in natural and spiritual knowledge. But being able to doesn't guarantee that they will. The more a Christian is renewed in his or her mind by the Word of God, the more that person will be able to discern spiritual knowledge. That includes wise counsel. Romans 8:6–7 says: "To be *carnally* minded is death, but to be *spiritually* minded is life and peace. Because the *carnal* mind is enmity against God; for it is *not subject to the law of God*, nor indeed can be.

Dealing with Pride

The second thing that can prevent a Christian from receiving wise counsel is pride. Rules 9 and 10 of the Twelve Rules of Knowledge are as follows:

9. Humility, like strength, enables you to climb the mountain of knowledge.

10. Pride, like gravity, prevents you from climbing the mountain of knowledge.

Pride will stop you from gaining knowledge at any level and category. The parable of the King and the Valley explains this well. You may remember that there are two brothers, Samuel and Eliab. Samuel, representing humility, climbs to the top of the mountain to gain the knowledge he needs. Eliab, representing pride, has no desire to climb the mountain and makes his decision based on personal convenience.

The higher up the mountain you go, the more you have to deal with the effects of gravity. The higher up the mountain of knowledge you go, the more you have to deal with pride, and pride can affect anybody, Christian and non-Christian alike.

A proud person refuses to learn from the hard blows, or lessons, of life. "Rebuke is more effective for a wise man than a hundred blows on a fool" (Proverbs 17:10). A humble person can receive wise counsel from anyone.

God is trying to get knowledge to you. Do you have your radar turned on? Remember. . . *you do not have a problem. You need more knowledge.*

I regularly examine myself to see if I am operating in pride. One of the primary ways in which I do this is by examining my willingness to receive wise counsel and instruction from others. Proverbs 9:8–9 says that a wise man loves instruction: "Do not correct a scoffer, lest he hate you; rebuke a wise man, and he will love you. Give instruction to a wise man, and he will be still wiser; teach a just man and he will increase in learning."

Where Do I Go for Wise Counsel?

God is trying to get knowledge to you so you can make wise decisions. His desire is for you to grow in observation, education, and revelation knowledge. If you are searching for knowledge, He will help you obtain the knowledge you need to be successful. That is only half of it, however. You still have to rightly apply that knowledge in order for your decisions to be wise. Remember that knowledge is everywhere, but wisdom is a *range of acquired knowledge rightly applied.* "Wisdom calls aloud outside; she raises her voice in the open squares. She cries out in the chief concourses, at the openings of the gates in the city she speaks her words" (Proverbs 1:20–21).

In this scripture, Solomon is illustrating how we obtain knowledge. *Wisdom* represents God. Wisdom's *voice* represents God speaking to you. It is not a coincidence, for example, that you are reading the information contained in this book. God had something to do with that. The *open squares* and *chief concourses* represent wherever people are found. The *city* represents you as an individual. The *gates* represent your senses through which you receive information from the outside world. The two primary gates through which you obtain knowledge are your eyes and ears. Notice it says that at the *openings* of the *gates* wisdom speaks her words. The openings represent open eyes and ears. Wisdom cries out to eyes and ears that are open and receptive.

In Proverbs 1:23 Solomon mentions the Holy Spirit or Spirit of Wisdom. "Surely I will pour out my spirit on you; I will make my words known to you."

God is endeavoring to get knowledge to us by various means. Our part is to be receptive to the range of knowledge out there and rightly apply it. I have observed that many people desire to grow in knowledge and wisdom but don't know where to go to get it. Remember, God is not trying to withhold wisdom from you. He wants you to gain wisdom and succeed in what He has called you to do!

First of all, God has strategically placed people in your path to speak wise counsel into your life. The Bible tells us that our steps are ordered of God. One of my favorite scriptures deals with this promise. "A man's steps are of the LORD; how then can a man understand his own way?" (Proverbs 20:24).

Since God is directing your steps, He must also have a diversity of counselors strategically placed to help you obtain wise counsel. He would not plan a successful life for you without the necessary advisors needed for you to win. Proverbs 15:22 says: "Without counsel, plans go awry, but in the *multitude of counselors* they are established." You see some of these people all the time, but you may not have considered them as a source of counsel until now. They include the following:

1. Family

2. Friends

3. Spiritual mentors

4. Individuals from other cultures

5. Members of the opposite sex

Receiving Council from Family

The family unit is part of God's design for you, and godly family members are a primary source of wise counsel. It is God's intent for spouses to help one another. Children and parents are also supposed to work together throughout their lives. Brothers, sisters, cousins, aunts, uncles, grandparents, and yes, even in-laws, can provide a wealth of wise council.

It amazes me that people will receive counsel from a virtual stranger and reject good advice from a caring family member.

Are you maximizing the wise counsel available to you through your family? Perhaps you do not come from a strong Christian family background. You may be the only Christian in your family right now. Don't let that discourage you. As a believer in Christ, you are part of an enormous family, the Body of Christ. The Bible tells us that the Lord sets the solitary in families. "God sets the solitary in families; He brings out those who are bound into prosperity; but the rebellious dwell in a dry land" (Psalm 68:6).

Solomon had a great deal to say about family dynamics regarding wise counsel. He emphasized the value of godly parents in counseling their children. In Proverbs 5:1–2 he says: "My son, pay attention to my wisdom; lend your ear to my understanding, that you may preserve discretion, and your lips may keep knowledge."

Five chapters in Proverbs begin with the words "my son" and deal with a parent giving counsel to his or her child. If it is so important for a child to heed wise counsel from a parent, how much more important should it be for us to heed our heavenly Father's counsel in His Word?

Let's talk about the family members God has placed in your life to help you acquire wise counsel for your decision making.

A Godly Spouse

A godly spouse is not only a gift from God but also a valuable asset. God gave Eve to Adam to be his helper. "The LORD God said, 'It is not good that man should be alone; I will make him a *helper* comparable to him'" (Genesis 2:18).

The Bible tells us that a virtuous wife is more valuable than precious stones. Almost all of Proverbs chapter 31 describes the value of a virtuous, godly wife. "Who can find a virtuous wife? For her worth is far above rubies" (Proverbs 31:10). Notice what else it says about a virtuous wife when she speaks: "She opens her mouth with wisdom, and on her tongue is the law of kindness" (Proverbs 31:26).

If you are married to a godly woman, I pray you do not take her for granted. Tell her how special she is and how much she means to you. The virtuous wife's husband does just that. Her children rise up and call her blessed; her husband also, and *he praises her.* "Many daughters have done well, but you excel them all" (Proverbs 31:28–29). Notice how her husband cherishes and praises his wife. He is saying to her, "Honey, you are the best of the best!" When was the last time you told your wife how special she is? If it has been awhile, you should take a moment to do so right now.

A godly husband is also a great blessing. Job is a good example. He was extremely prosperous in his finances, his family life, and his relationship with God. We often think of Job as a very wealthy man. Did you know he was also highly regarded for his wisdom? "Men listened to me and waited, and kept silence for my counsel. After my words they did not speak again, and my speech settled on them as dew" (Job 29:21–22). Wouldn't you like that to be said of you? I certainly would!

One of God's greatest blessings to you is a godly spouse. I am referring to a God-fearing and Bible-believing husband or wife. A godly spouse can speak into your life better than anyone because he or she knows you better than anyone. Your spouse knows your strengths, weaknesses, dreams, and aspirations. A godly spouse can give you wise counsel twenty-four hours a day. Don't ever exclude your spouse when making a big decision. God designed your spouse's counsel to be part of your decision making, providing you with a perspective that he or she is uniquely qualified to give.

A prudent spouse is a blessing from God. "Houses and riches are an inheritance from fathers, but a *prudent* wife is from the LORD" (Proverbs 19:14). *Webster's College Dictionary* defines *prudent* as "marked by wisdom, shrewdly practical, circumspect, discreet." My wife Libby is a remarkable lady. She never ceases to amaze me with her insights and perspectives. Many times she will confirm what I believe I am supposed to do in a particular situation. It's astonishing how two people of the opposite sex, from different backgrounds, can come together and regularly agree on decisions. God's plan is for you and your spouse to be one, and that includes areas of decision making.

Perhaps you are married and your relationship with your wife is not like that described in scripture. Love your spouse and pray for them. Let them see Jesus in you. I am not saying you should remain in a relationship where there is infidelity or abuse. In such situations you need to get help. Choosing a godly spouse is one of the most important decisions you will ever make. Ladies, you want to marry a Boaz, not a Bozo. Men, you want to marry a Ruth, not a Ruthless.

Your Children

Raising a family God's way has great rewards. One of the benefits is wise children. It is gratifying as a father to hear your children teach you something from God's Word and give you advice. I enjoy discussing situations with my children and asking them for their opinions. They have the perspective of the next generation. My daughters will give advice to me straight, not sugar-coated, giving me an opportunity to see things from a different perspective. Like my wife, they often confirm what I am thinking.

Children are a blessing from the Lord, and when they are older, that includes decision making. As it says in Psalm 128:1 and 3, "Blessed is every one who fears the LORD, who walks in His ways. . . . Your wife shall be like a fruitful vine in the very heart of your house, *your children* like olive plants all around your table."

Extended Family (Jethro's Visit)

In Exodus 18 Jethro visited his son-in-law Moses when he was encamped with the children of Israel in the wilderness. The next day Jethro noticed that Moses sat from morning to evening as judge for the people. He called Moses to him and said:

> *"The thing that you do is not good. Both you and these people who are with you will surely wear yourselves out. For this thing is too much for you; you are not able to perform it by yourself. Listen now to my voice; I will give you counsel, and God will be with you" (Exodus 18:17–19).*

Jethro instructed Moses to appoint able men to be rulers of thousands, hundreds, fifties, and tens to judge the smaller matters. The more difficult cases would be brought to Moses. "Moses *heeded the voice of his father-in-law* and did all that he had said" (Exodus 18:24). "Then Moses let his father-in-law depart, and he went his way to his own land" (Exodus 18:27).

God could have given Moses this advice directly by the Holy Spirit. Instead He sent an extended family member with wise counsel to help him. This is part of God's decision-making process. Sometimes we want a word from the Lord when God is sending us a Jethro. Moses humbled himself and cooperated with God's process. You can have similar results when you do the same.

Extended Family (Jehonathan and Joab)

In 1 Chronicles 27 we are given a detailed account of David's governmental organization. His uncle Jehonathan is named as one of David's counselors, along with his sons. "Jehonathan, David's uncle, was a counselor, a wise man, and a scribe. . . . And the general of the king's army was Joab" (vv. 32, 34). Joab, King David's chief military commander and advisor, was also his nephew. He was the son of David's sister Zeruiah.

Receiving Counsel from Friends

You must choose your friends carefully. Their advice will either elevate or lower you. A godly friend will be faithful to give you good advice when needed. Proverbs 27:9 says: "Ointment and perfume delight the heart, and the sweetness of a man's friend gives delight by hearty *counsel.*"

People will sometimes heed poor advice from their friends because of personal ties. Remember, wisdom is a range of acquired knowledge that is rightly applied. Wisdom is not based on emotional ties with people. Emotions can be deceiving. Make sure your friends are wise and well grounded in God's Word.

Don't get rid of a friend who corrects you in love. A true friend may correct you on occasion. You need people like that in your life. "Faithful are the wounds of a friend, but the kisses of an enemy are deceitful" (Proverbs 27:6). I have seen relationships ruined because a person would not swallow his or her pride and receive godly counsel. You have stopped climbing the mountain of knowledge if you reject gentle rebukes from friends.

The Bible tells us that wise people appreciate correction and instruction from others. Proverbs 25:12 says: "Like an earring of gold and an ornament of fine gold is a wise rebuker to an obedient ear." In Proverbs 9:8 we read a similar message: "Do not correct a scoffer, lest he hate you; rebuke a wise man, and he will love you."

Rehoboam's Folly

In 1 Kings 12:1–17 and 2 Chronicles 10:1–17 we read the story of Rehoboam, Solomon's son, going to Shechem to be made king. Jeroboam, whom the prophet Ahijah said would rule over ten of the tribes of Israel, was there also. Jeroboam and the whole assembly told Rehoboam they would serve him if he lightened the burdensome taxes imposed by his father Solomon. Rehoboam instructed them to give him three days for his reply. So far so good.

Rehoboam consulted two groups of people for advice on how to reply to the assembly of Israel. The elders who were with his father Solomon advised as follows: "If you will be a servant to these people today, and serve them, and answer them, and speak good words to them, then they will be your servants forever" (1 Kings 12:7).

One of the amazing things about this story is that Solomon, the wisest man ever, had advisors as well. You and I will never reach the point where we won't need the counsel of others. The Bible says that Rehoboam rejected the advice given to him by the elders. He then consulted young men who had grown up with him. The young men advised that he reply to the people as follows: "My little finger shall be thicker than my father's waist! And now, whereas my father put a heavy yoke on you, I will add to your yoke; my father chastised you with whips, but I will chastise you with scourges" (1 Kings 12:10–11).

Rehoboam rejected the advice from the wise elders. He listened instead to the poor advice from his friends. That mistake would cost him dearly. Rehoboam spoke roughly to the people and ten of the tribes rejected his leadership. Jeroboam was made ruler over the ten tribes instead, dividing the kingdom to Israel in the north and Judah in the south.

Rehoboam's poor decision to reject the advice of the wise and listen to his friends instead left him with clouded judgment. Choose your friends carefully. They will help keep you on the right track. Proverbs 12:26 says: "The righteous should choose his friends carefully, for the way of the wicked leads them astray."

You may be convinced that you need to choose your friends carefully but are wondering where you can find the kind of friends that will give you wise counsel when you need it. A good place to begin is in your local church. "Those who are planted in the house of the LORD shall flourish in the courts of our God" (Psalm 92:13).

Webster's College Dictionary defines the verb *plant* as "to put or set in the ground to grow, to cause to become established." In 1 Timothy 3:15 Paul calls the local church the pillar and *ground* of the truth. When you are planted in the local church, you will grow in every area of your life. In this case, planted means being involved in what your local church is doing. God will direct you to the church you are supposed to be in, and also show you where you are to serve and bear fruit. Trees that are planted bear fruit.

By being involved and serving in your local church, you will develop godly friendships. These are the kinds of friends that will be able to give you wise counsel. By being around people of like faith and passion you will find others whom God is taking in the same direction He is taking you. They will be able to speak into your life. This commitment will require a willingness on your part to invest time, energy, and resources.

I love serving in the local church. I have served as a parking-lot attendant, usher-greeter, custodian, children's-church worker, cell-group leader, Japanese church worker, audio assistant, Spanish translator, choir member, prison-ministry volunteer, and physician for medical emergencies. During my service in these areas, I have developed relationships with people. I am able to speak into their lives and they do the same for me. This is part of God's program for your spiritual growth. If you want to grow in wisdom, you have to be involved in your local church. Everyone has a vital role in their local body of believers. Ephesians 4:16 says: "From whom the whole body, joined and knit together *by what every joint supplies*, according to the effective working by which every part does its share, *causes growth of the body* for the edifying of itself in love."

Keep in mind that God's plan for you to grow in wisdom is not all about you. God's design is for you and others around you to grow for the purpose of helping others. You and I are called to a life of service.

Spiritual Mentors

It's often possible to find a good spiritual mentor in your local church as well. A good example of this is Saul of Tarsus, who later became the apostle Paul. He came from a very religious background but did not encounter Jesus until he was traveling to the city of Damascus. The men he was with saw nothing, but Paul saw a light so bright it blinded him and he spoke with Jesus. Finally convinced that Jesus was the risen Messiah, Paul's life changed drastically. He was given refuge in a Christian home, where he was prayed for and healed of his blindness. Barnabas took Paul under his wing during the early days of his ministry, and Paul became active in the church at Antioch. During his missionary journeys, he had significant interaction with other Christian leaders, including Peter and James the Lord's brother. He met these men because he became part of the church.

Proverbs 13:20 speaks of the principle of mentoring: "He who walks with wise men will be wise, but the companion of fools will be destroyed." You will become like the people you spend time with. That's true in both a negative and positive sense. Align yourself with wise people—those who can mentor you—and you are sure to gain wisdom. Do you know what Joshua, Samuel, Elisha, Esther, Timothy, and Peter all had in common? They all had a God-ordained mentor. Look at these scriptures and see for yourself.

Joshua Had Moses

> The LORD *said to Moses,* "Come up to Me on the mountain *and be there; and I will give you tablets of stone, and the law and commandments which I have written, that you may teach them.*" So Moses arose **with his assistant** Joshua, *and Moses went up to the mountain of God (Exodus 24:12–13).*

> Joshua the son of Nun was full of the spirit of wisdom, for Moses *had laid his hands on him; so the children of Israel heeded him, and did as the* LORD *had commanded Moses (Deuteronomy 34:9).*

Samuel Had Eli

> Samuel ministered before the LORD, *even as a child (1 Samuel 2:18).*

> **The boy** Samuel ministered to the LORD *before Eli. . . . So Samuel* **grew,** *and the* LORD *was with him and let none of his words fall to the ground. And all Israel from Dan to Beersheba knew*

that Samuel had been established as a prophet of the LORD (1 Samuel 3:1, 19–20).

Elisha Had Elijah

[Elijah] departed from there, and found Elisha the son of Shaphat, who was plowing with twelve yoke of oxen before him, and he was with the twelfth. Then Elijah passed by him and threw his mantle on him (1 Kings 19:19).

[Elisha] arose and followed Elijah, and became his servant (1 Kings 19:21).

Suddenly a chariot of fire appeared with horses of fire, and separated the two of them; and Elijah went up by a whirlwind into heaven. . . . Then [Elisha] took the mantle of Elijah that had fallen from him, and struck the water, and said, "Where is the LORD God of Elijah?" And when he also had struck the water, it was divided this way and that; and Elisha crossed over (2 Kings 2:11, 14).

Esther Had Mordecai

Mordecai had brought up Hadassah, that is, Esther, his uncle's daughter, for she had neither father nor mother. The young woman was lovely and beautiful. When her father and mother died, Mordecai took her as his own daughter (Esther 2:7).

Esther had not revealed her family and her people, just as Mordecai had charged her, for Esther obeyed the command of Mordecai as when she was brought up by him (Esther 2:20).

Timothy Had Paul

> *[Paul] came to Derbe and Lystra. And behold, a certain disciple was there, named Timothy. . . . He was well spoken of by the brethren who were at Lystra and Iconium. Paul wanted to have him go on with him (Acts 16:1–3).*

Peter Had Jesus

> *Jesus, walking by the Sea of Galilee, saw two brothers, Simon called Peter, and Andrew his brother, casting a net into the sea; for they were fishermen. Then He said to them, "Follow Me, and I will make you fishers of men" (Mathew 4:18–19).*

> *When they saw the boldness of Peter and John, and perceived that they were uneducated and untrained men, they marveled. And they realized that they had been with Jesus (Acts 4:13).*

Spiritual mentors come in a variety of shapes and sizes, as you can see from these examples. They may come from different generations, like Eli and Samuel or Moses and Joshua. They may be relatives, like Mordecai and Esther. They may have similar callings, like Elijah and Elisha. They may have different cultural backgrounds, like Paul and Timothy. They may have different vocations, like Jesus the carpenter's son, and Peter the fisherman. God has strategically placed a variety of spiritual mentors in your life to help you learn, grow, and fulfill your destiny.

The Lord has blessed me with mentors who have helped me along the way. Each one has had something special to offer. I thank God for them. Remember, God wants you to grow in wisdom and succeed even more than you do. He has mentors

for you as you seek Him and remain humble. And remember
. . . every Christian has Jesus, the greatest mentor of all, living inside. Hebrews 13:5–6 says: "He Himself has said, "'I will
never leave you nor forsake you.'

So we may boldly say: 'The LORD is my helper; I will not fear.
What can man do to me?' "

Individuals from Other Cultures

We human beings have a tendency to mistrust those who
look, think, and act differently than we do. This practice limits
us, for meeting those from other cultures and nationalities can
widen our perspective and understanding of the world.

I believe Solomon was talking about a cultural diversity *and*
numbers when he mentioned a multitude of counselors. Proverbs 15:22 says: "Without counsel, plans go awry, but in the
multitude of counselors they are established."

Moses, a Hebrew, was educated in the knowledge of the
Egyptians. God used that educational background to help
Moses lead the children of Israel out of bondage. "Moses was
learned in all the wisdom *of the Egyptians*, and was mighty in
words and deeds" (Acts 7:22).

Your ability to acquire knowledge will be limited if you
exclude people from other cultures. Look around. If you limit
your range of knowledge to your generation, gender, ethnic
background, and economic status, you are limiting what God
can do in your life. Pride has to be dealt with. Acts 7:22 is referring to the natural knowledge Moses acquired from the Egyptians. The same principle applies to wise, godly counsel. No

culture has the monopoly on spiritual knowledge from God. Moses was a Hebrew. His closest advisors, his wife Zipporah and father-in-law Jethro, were Midianites.

The United States military is strong because of its diversity. There are superiors, male and female, from many ethnic backgrounds. Everyone brings something special to the table. If the military can make it work, so can the Body of Christ. Is there diversity in your team or does everyone look the same? Diversity makes you stronger, not weaker. Proverbs 24:6 says: "By wise counsel you will wage your own war, and in a multitude of counselors there is safety."

Members of the Opposite Sex

Deborah was one of twelve judges mentioned in the book of Judges. She was unique among the judges in that she was a female. "Deborah, a prophetess, the wife of Lapidoth, was judging Israel at that time. And she would sit under the palm tree of Deborah between Ramah and Bethel in the mountains of Ephraim. And *the children of Israel* came up to her for judgment" (Judges 4:4–5).

She was a prophetess, anointed and empowered by God to be the spiritual and political leader for the nation. Notice that the scripture says that *the children of Israel* came up to her for judgment. That means the entire nation, male and female, sought her out for her wisdom and counsel.

Men, do you have a hard time receiving knowledge and counsel from women? Ladies, do you have a hard time receiving knowledge and counsel from men? I am speaking about knowledge and counsel given in an appropriate setting. I encourage you to examine yourself. Is there any gender bias or pride that prevents you from acquiring wisdom from someone of the opposite sex? If you are going to climb higher in wisdom, you have to get past this ledge in your thinking. To believe that your gender is somehow intellectually superior is foolishness.

A professional colleague once told me the reason God made Deborah a judge was that He could not find a man to do the job. I almost laughed. I didn't mean to be disrespectful to my friend, as he sincerely believed what he was saying. I guess the Lord was able to turn Gideon from a coward into a mighty man of valor and judge, but Lapidoth was just too hard of a nut for Him to crack! He had to use Deborah, his wife, instead. The fact is God calls and uses whom He chooses.

God uses men and women mightily in the area of counsel and wisdom. God gives wisdom liberally to all who ask, men and women alike, and without reproach. James 1:5 says: "If any of you lacks wisdom, let him ask of God, who gives to *all* liberally and without reproach, and it will be given to him."

I have spiritual brothers and dads as well as spiritual sisters and moms. I thank God for them all. You can gain an abundance of wise counsel from someone of the opposite sex if you are willing to humble yourself. As Galatians 3:28 says: "There is neither Jew nor Greek, there is neither slave nor free, *there is neither male nor female*; for you are all one in Christ Jesus."

We have now learned about Step #4, which is making a wise decision. This included the following:

• A definition of godly advice for making life decisions

- The line of demarcation, or barrier, between the third and fourth categories of knowledge

- Knowledge is broken up into six categories. The first three deal with natural knowledge. Four through six deal with spiritual knowledge.

- Wise counsel can be obtained through godly relationships with your family, friends, spiritual mentors, individuals from other cultures, and members of the opposite sex. Pride has to be dealt with in order to receive wise counsel from any of these groups of people.

There are seven questions you have to ask yourself when making a wise decision. These are the questions we have covered so far:

Question #1—What have I learned from personal successes and mistakes?

Question #2—What have I learned from others' successes and mistakes?

Question #3—What have I learned from technical knowledge?

Question #4—What have I learned from wise counsel?

Once you have answered questions 1–4, you are ready to move on to the third and highest level of knowledge and Steps 5 and 6 in making a wise decision. You are now approaching the summit of knowledge and wisdom. This is where it really gets exciting.

Discussion

1. What is the fourth category of knowledge?

2. Where is the line of demarcation between natural knowledge and spiritual knowledge?

3. Explain the difference between the natural, the spiritual, and the carnal man.

4. Why can't the natural and carnal man receive wise counsel?

5. What are the two primary reasons mentioned in this chapter why people do not receive wise counsel?

6. Fill in the blanks. What are the five categories of people capable of giving us wise, godly counsel?

   F_____

   F_____

   S_____ M_____

   I_____ F__ O____ C_____

   M_____ O_ T__ O_____ S__

CHAPTER 9

Revelation: The Third Level of Knowledge

Proverbs 15:31–33 is the foundational passage for this teaching on decision making. Verse 33 speaks about the third level of knowledge, which is revelation knowledge. Revelation knowledge comes from the Lord. "The fear *of the* Lord is the instruction of wisdom, and before honor is humility."

Revelation knowledge is broken down into the fifth and sixth categories of knowledge or learning:

Category #5: learning from the Word of God

Category #6: learning from the Holy Spirit

What Is Revelation Knowledge?

Revelation knowledge is not a mysterious, nebulous concept. On the contrary, it is the basis for our relationship with God, the creator of the universe. Revelation knowledge is God communicating with us. Let's look at three important scriptures:

The Lord *gives wisdom; **from His mouth** come knowledge and understanding (Proverbs 2:6).*

*Have you heard **the counsel of God**? Do you limit wisdom to yourself? (Job 15:8).*

*Truly your God is the God of gods, the Lord of kings, and **a revealer of secrets**, since you could reveal this secret (Daniel 2:47).*

Webster's College Dictionary defines *revelation* as "an act of revealing or communicating divine truth." The word for revelation in the Bible is the Greek word *apokalupsis* (Strong's # 602) from which we get the word *apocalypse. Apokalupsis* means "an uncovering." The book of Apokalupsis or Revelation refers to the Revelation of Jesus Christ. The Lord Jesus is at the heart of revelation knowledge. We read in Revelation 1:1: "The Revelation of Jesus Christ, *which God gave* Him, to show His servants—things which must shortly take place. And He sent and signified it by His angel to His servant John."

Revelation knowledge comes directly from the throne room of God to the heart of man. The word *apokalupsis* occurs twelve times in the New Testament, all in the letters to the Church. The Lord gave me two scriptural definitions for revelation knowledge. Both definitions are based on Paul's prayers in his letter to the church at Ephesus. The first definition is more comprehensive. The second definition is simple and easy to remember.

The first scriptural definition of revelation knowledge comes from Paul's prayer in Ephesians 1:15–19:

Therefore I also, after I heard of your faith in the Lord Jesus and your love for all the saints, do not cease to give thanks for you, making mention of you in my prayers: that the God of our Lord Jesus Christ, the Father of glory, may give to you the spirit of wisdom and revelation in the knowledge of Him, the eyes of your understanding being enlightened; that you may know what is the hope of His calling, what are the riches of the glory of His inheritance in the saints, and what is the exceeding greatness of His power toward us who believe, according to the working of His mighty power.

The scriptural definition of revelation knowledge from Ephesians chapter 1 can be expressed this way: believing, understanding, and experiencing God's person, knowledge, and power by the Holy Spirit.

Paul again prays for the church to have revelation knowledge in Ephesians 3: 14–19:

For this reason I bow my knees to the Father of our Lord Jesus Christ, from whom the whole family in heaven and earth is named, that He would grant you, according to the riches of His glory, to be strengthened with might through His Spirit in the inner man, that Christ may dwell in your hearts through faith; that you, being rooted and grounded in love, may be able to comprehend with all the saints what is the width and length and depth and height—to know the love of Christ which passes knowledge; that you may be filled with all the fullness of God.

A similar scriptural definition of revelation knowledge, this time from Ephesians chapter 3, can be expressed this way: knowing and experiencing God.

Let's review what we've learned from God's Word about revelation:

- Revelation is received by faith in Jesus Christ.

- Revelation is both *knowing and understanding Jesus Christ and His ways.*

- Revelation is *experiencing the power of God* in your being through the Holy Spirit.

- Revelation knowledge is *knowing and experiencing God.*

- Revelation knowledge transforms your spirit, soul, and body into the image of Christ.

How to Receive Revelation Knowledge

Revelation knowledge is God communicating directly to you supernaturally. He does so in two ways: through His Word (the Bible) and through His Spirit. When you humble yourself and learn how to operate in observation and education knowledge, you will be able to handle revelation knowledge without stumbling. You have now become an expert climber. You will have to invest the greatest amount of time, energy, and resources to get to this level. There is no pride in revelation knowledge. Neither the natural man nor the carnal man can receive the things of God. Only the spiritual man can receive the things of God. Humility must rule. Do you remember the lesson we learned from the King and the Valley?

In order to stand on the mountain peak called Wisdom where the clouds dwell, the eagles soar, and the view is the most spectacular, you must begin climbing the mountain of Knowledge at its base.

You are now ready to enter the realm of revelation knowledge where the clouds dwell, the eagles soar, and the view is the most spectacular.

Discussion

1. What is the third level of knowledge?

2. What are the fifth and sixth categories of knowledge?

3. What are the two ways in which God communicates revelation knowledge to us?

4. What does the Greek word for revelation, *apokalupsis*, mean?

5. True or false:

   • The natural man can receive the things of God.

   • The carnal man can receive the things of God.

   • The spiritual man can receive the things of God.

   • Revelation knowledge is God communicating directly to man in a supernatural way.

   • Revelation knowledge is more than just head knowledge. It is believing, understanding, and experiencing God's person, knowledge, and power by the Holy Spirit.

   • Revelation knowledge is knowing and experiencing God.

   • There is no pride in revelation knowledge. Humility must rule.

STEP #5: LEARNING FROM THE WORD OF GOD

The fear of the Lord is the instruction of wisdom,
and before honor is humility.—Proverbs 15:33

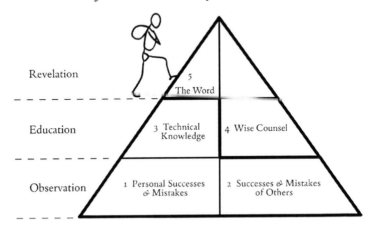

Revelation
5 The Word

Education
3 Technical Knowledge   4 Wise Counsel

Observation
1 Personal Successes & Mistakes   2 Successes & Mistakes of Others

The Word Is a Person, Alive and Powerful

Your life will be revolutionized when you fully understand that the Word of God is a person, Jesus Christ. John 1:1 says: "In the beginning was the Word, and the Word was with God, and the Word was God." And that's not all! If the Word of God is a person, Jesus Christ, then the Word of God is alive! Look at John 1:14: "The Word became flesh and dwelt among us, and we beheld His glory, the glory as of the only begotten of the Father, full of grace and truth."

Furthermore, if the Word of God is Jesus Christ, and the Word of God is alive, then the Word of God is powerful. Hebrews 4:12 says: "The word of God is living and powerful, and sharper than any two-edged sword."

The Word of God is not just a book. The Word of God is Jesus Christ, the son of almighty God. Jesus, the Word, became flesh. He paid the price for our sins on the cross so that we may have eternal life through faith in Him. He rose from the dead and is seated at the right hand of the Father. All authority has been given to Him in heaven and on earth. The Word is Jesus Christ. The Word is alive. The Word is powerful.

The Word of God is living and powerful because Jesus is living and powerful. If you are a Christian, He lives in you. When you read and confess God's Word you are reading and confessing absolute truth and power. You were created to speak the Word of God with power.

Listen, O coastlands, to Me, and take heed, you peoples from afar! The LORD has called Me from the womb; from the matrix of My mother He has made mention of My name. And He has made My mouth like a sharp sword; in the shadow of His hand He has hidden Me, and made Me a polished shaft; in His quiver He has hidden Me (Isaiah 49:1–2).

The Word: Food for Your Spirit, Soul, and Body

You are a three-part being made in the image of God. You have a spirit, soul, and body, and the Word of God is food for all of them, just like food is nourishment to your physical body. Jesus said we are to live our lives sustained by the bread of God's Word. "He answered and said, 'It is written, "Man shall not live by bread alone, but by every word that proceeds from the mouth of God" ' " (Matthew 4:4).

How much time do you spend each day feeding your physical body? An hour? If you spend an hour a day feeding your body with natural food, how much time should you spend each day feeding your spirit with God's supernatural Word?

Perhaps you are in a season where you don't have much time for studying God's Word. I know this feeling very well. There were times in my medical career when I had to choose between eating lunch or spending half an hour in God's Word that day. There were call nights when I knew I was only going to get three hours of sleep. I would still try to give God His thirty minutes that day. Half an hour was my line in the sand. There were many nights when I fell asleep on my office couch with my Bible on my chest. I know the Lord honored that sacrifice, because now I have more time to study His Word than ever before. The Lord honors those who honor Him. I decided a long time ago I would rather sacrifice food or sleep than miss out on the powerful, spiritual food contained in His Word. Job said it like this: "I have treasured the words of His mouth more than necessary food" (Job 23:12).

A person who runs out of food will lose energy and become weaker. A car that runs out of gas will come to a halt. A plane that runs out of fuel will have to make an emergency landing. It is important for Christians to feed their spirits with the Word of God regularly. Otherwise they will become weak, come to a halt, or lose control and have to make an emergency landing. God's Word contains a limitless supply of life and power. Make time daily to feed your spirit with God's Word. You will experience victory in your life like never before if you keep your spirit well fed. "Jesus said to them, 'I am the bread of life. He who comes to Me shall never hunger, and he who believes in Me shall never thirst'" (John 6:35).

The Parable of the Sword

In Hebrews 4:12 we read that the Word of God is living and powerful and sharper than any two-edged sword. A person is like a sword based on how much knowledge and revelation of God's Word they have in them. The extent of the *logos*, or written Word, in you gives the sword its length. The extent of the *rhema*, or the revealed Word, in you gives the sword its sharpness, its power. There are four types of people when it comes to the Word of God.

- **The first person: little logos/little rhema.** These are people with little written Word in them and little revelation of that Word. They believe in Jesus as their savior, but they do not study the Bible regularly to grow spiritually. They walk around defeated because they do not know what Christ has done for them. These people are like plastic knives—short and not very sharp. The devil is not afraid of people like this. An example of this would be a Christian who is still trying to earn his or her salvation through good works, when Ephesians 2:8 tells us we are saved by grace, through faith.

- **The second person: little logos/much rhema.** These are people with little written Word in them but much revelation of that Word. They have victory in some areas of their life where there is revelation, such as healing, finances, and spiritual authority. These people are like hunting knives—short but very sharp. The devil is more cautious of these people. An example would be Christians who understand salvation by grace through faith, and healing, but do not understand prosperity, authority of the believer, or gifts of the Holy Spirit. They are strong Christians but are missing out on the fullness of what God has for them in other areas of life.

The third person: much logos/little rhema. These are people with much written Word in them but little revelation of that Word. They know what the Word says but they don't believe it for lack of revelation. They know about Jesus, but they don't know Jesus. They don't have a relationship with Him. They have no victory in their lives because the Bible is not a living reality for them. These people are like plastic swords—long and blunt. They pose no threat. The devil is not afraid of these people. An example of this might be those who teach religion at a secular university, to which Jesus is just a historical figure and not the living Son of God.

The fourth person: much logos/much rhema. These are people with much written Word in them and much revelation of that Word. They know what the Word of God says, and they believe it by faith. They have victory in all areas of life because they are both hearers and doers of the Word. These people are like battle swords—long and very sharp. The devil is terrified of these Christians.

The logos (written Word in you) gives the sword its length, and the rhema (revealed Word in you) gives the sword its sharpness, its power. And what the devil is afraid of more than anything else is when the Word of God and the Spirit of God come together in a man or woman created in the image of God.

Ephesians 6:17 calls the Word of God the sword of the Spirit. You are responsible for getting the written Word in you and lengthening your sword. The Holy Spirit is responsible for revealing the Word in you and sharpening your sword. Do not become discouraged if nothing appears to be happening right away. Just as it takes time to hammer and sharpen a natural sword, so it takes time to sharpen the spiritual sword of God's Word in your heart.

The devil knows he is defeated when the Word of God comes alive in your heart. Nothing terrifies him more than a believer who lives by revelation knowledge of God's Word. The Word of God is working on the inside of you. As you diligently seek God in His Word He promises to do His part. Hebrews 11:6, the scripture that changed my life, says that God is a rewarder of those who *diligently* seek Him. You must be diligent when studying God's Word. How much time should you invest studying God's Word? *You study God's Word until rhema comes.* Growing in revelation knowledge is a partnership between you and the Lord.

The Map and the Compass

Your life is a journey, and on that journey you need a map and a compass. The Word is your map and the Holy Spirit is your compass. Without a map you are either going nowhere or you don't know where you are going. In the military you would never think of going to war without intelligence from a map. It is no different for you and me. A map tells you:

- Where you are and what your destination is;

- About the terrain you are in;

- Where the obstacles are and how to negotiate them;

- The easiest and most difficult paths to take;

- Where the enemy will most likely attack;

- How long it may take to reach your objective;

- Where the high ground is located.

I hope by the Spirit of God you are hearing what I am saying. You must become familiar with your map—the Word of God— if you are going to be victorious in your theater of operations.

Revelation Knowledge Is a Way of Life

The book of Psalms is one of the five wisdom books in the bible. It is a book of praise and worship to God. Many Christian songs contain passages found in the Psalms. The first psalm, however, has nothing to do with praise and worship. It has to do with the Word of God, specifically the first three verses. It is a passage I meditate on every day of my life:

Blessed is the man who walks not in the counsel of the ungodly, nor stands in the path of sinners, nor sits in the seat of the scornful; but his delight is in the law of the LORD, and in His law he meditates day and night. He shall be like a tree planted by the rivers of water, that brings forth its fruit in its season, whose leaf also shall not wither; and whatever he does shall prosper (Psalm 1:1–3).

I used to wonder why the first psalm was not about praise and worship when almost all the other psalms are. The Lord explained to me one of the reasons for this. He said: *"Son, you cannot love someone you do not know. People love Me to the degree that they know Me."*

The more you meditate on God's Word, the more you will know Him and His love for you. Your love for Him will naturally grow as well. In Mark 12:29–30 Jesus said the first of all commandments is to love the Lord your God with all your heart, soul, mind, and strength. You are able to do this by knowing God first through His Word and then by His Spirit.

The Hebrew word for meditate in Psalm 1:2 is the word *hagah* (Strong's # 1897). This word means "to meditate, moan, growl, utter, speak." This word means to think about something in earnest, *often with the focus on future plans and contingencies,* possibly speaking to God or oneself in low tones. Meditating on God's Word is part of wise decision making.

Revelation knowledge is a way of life. There are three steps to becoming the prosperous, fruitful person described in Psalm 1:1–3. The first two steps are your responsibility. The third step is automatic.

STEP #1: CONSECRATION

Blessed is the man who walks not in the counsel of the ungodly, nor stands in the path of sinners, nor sits in the seat of the scornful.—Psalm 1:1

Step #2: Preparation

But his delight is in the law of the LORD, and in
His law he meditates day and night.—Psalm 1:2

Step #3: Multiplication

He shall be like a tree planted by the rivers of
water, that brings forth its fruit in its season,
whose leaf also shall not wither; and whatever he
does shall prosper.—Psalm 1:3

Read verse 3 again. You represent the *tree*. The word *planted* has a dual meaning. It means to be planted or established in God's Word and the local church where God's Word is proclaimed. The *rivers* of water represent the abundant, fresh, continuous, and life-giving supply of revelation knowledge from God's Word. The tree *roots* represent roots of faith, buried deep in the ground and continually fed by the river no matter what season you are in. The soil where roots of faith take hold represents your heart. Jesus used this illustration in the parable of the soils (Matthew 13:1–23; Mark 4:1–20; Luke 8:4–15). God *promises* that people like this will bring forth fruit in season. The *fruit* represents the fruit of the Spirit (Galatians 5:22–23) and gifts of the Spirit (1 Corinthians 12:1–11), as well as the talents (Proverbs 18:16) God has placed within you to glorify Him. The *leaf*, or anointing, will not wither, and whatever you do will prosper. God promises all of this to you through a lifestyle of consecration and revelation.

The Word of God Will Speak with You

If you meditate on God's Word long enough, it will speak to you. Proverbs 6:20–22 says: "My son, keep your father's command, and do not forsake the law of your mother. Bind them continually upon your heart; tie them around your neck. When you roam, they will lead you; when you sleep, they will keep you; and when you awake, they *will speak with you.*" Yes, that's right, speak to you!

Remember, Jesus is the Word. God will speak to you first through His Word. If what you are hearing doesn't line up with God's Word, the Bible, it's not God. The devil also has a message for you, one that can destroy your life if you listen to it. This is why it's so important to get the Word of God in you. It will help you determine what is truth and what is counterfeit. In John 8:31–32 Jesus says that if you abide in His Word you will know the truth and the truth will make you free. Free from what? Free from the works of the devil. God *can* speak to you through His Word. God *wants* to speak to you through His Word. God *will* speak to you through His Word.

The Word of God and the Spirit of God have the same voice. Once you have learned to recognize God's voice in His Word, it will be easy for you to recognize the leading voice of His Spirit. Jesus, the living Word, said this: "My sheep hear My voice, and I know them, and they follow Me" (John 10:27). Fellowship with your heavenly Father is not only talking to Him, but also listening to Him. "There are many plans in a man's heart, nevertheless the LORD's counsel—that will stand" (Proverbs 19:21).

God wants you to be led by the counsel of His Word and His Spirit. For example, in writing this book, the Lord has not only told me what scriptures to use but also confirmed over and over the word He has given me. I received two confirmations the day I wrote down the teaching from Psalm 1:1–3 that I just gave you. Libby received a thank-you note later that day from our pastor quoting Psalm 1:3.

Also that evening, I decided to read Psalm 52 before going to bed. I do not routinely read this psalm, nor am I familiar with it. At first I didn't want to read it because it deals with David's enemies trying to destroy him. This wasn't exactly what I was hoping for right before going to sleep. I started looking for another psalm when the Lord urged me to stay and read the whole thing. I understood why He did when I got to verse 8, the next to last verse. "I am *like a green olive tree in the house of God; I trust in the mercy of God forever and ever*" (Psalm 52:8).

This verse also references the teaching on Psalm 1:3 in regard to being planted in the local church. God was again confirming His Word to me. God is that precise about communicating His Word to you. This may seem quirky for someone who is not used to being led by the Word and Spirit of God. This becomes more natural with increased sensitivity to His voice. There are many things I could say, but I want to write down what the Lord is saying. Staying tuned in to His voice allows you to do that.

When the Lord gives you a word He expects you to do something with it. When you obey His word, in faith, He will confirm that word. If it's God's Word, He will confirm it. You can have absolute confidence that you are doing His will when He gives you a word, you obey, and He confirms His word. The Word of God will speak with you.

Identification: Seeing Yourself in the Bible

The principle of identification is crucial to effective decision making. The Bible is a treasure chest of stories to help you with the situations and decisions in your life. Do you identify with some of the characters in the Bible when you are going through a particular situation? That's what God is hoping you will do. The Scriptures tell us that stories in the Bible are to serve as examples from which we can learn kingdom principles. 1 Corinthians 10:11 says: "All these things happened to them *as examples*, and they were written for our admonition, upon whom the ends of the ages have come" (1 Corinthians 10:11).

Job is someone we can all identify with at some point in our lives. Everyone has been through some form of adversity. Sometimes people say things like, "Why is this happening to me?" or "God, I can't take this anymore." James helps us understand that suffering produces patience in us, helping to mold our character. We also see that God, who is compassionate and merciful, intends for us to have a good end similar to Job. James 5:10–11 says:

My brethren, take the prophets, who spoke in the name of Lord, as an example of suffering and patience. Indeed we count them blessed who endure. You have heard of the perseverance of Job and seen the end intended by the Lord—that the Lord is very compassionate and merciful.

188 the art of decision

Whenever we read a story in the Bible, we should try to learn from other people's experiences. It should become something we do automatically. The Bible teaches us to learn from its characters. "Whatever things were written before were written for our learning, that we through the patience and comfort of the Scriptures might have hope" (Romans 15:4).

Genesis 25:29–34 tells us how Esau sold his birthright to his brother Jacob for a bowl of stew. Esau had just come in from the field and was weary. Esau made a terrible decision when he was hungry and tired. Sometimes when I come home after caring for patients all night Libby asks me to make a big decision. I am often weary and hungry when I arrive, just like Esau was when he made his error. I eat some food and tell Libby I will make a decision after I wake up from a nap. Seeing yourself in the Bible is part of the decision-making process.

In John 13:3–17 we read the account of Jesus washing His disciples' feet, leaving us an example of being a servant. John 13:15 says: "I have given you an *example*, that you should do as I have done to you." The Bible has an explanation and answer for every situation in life.

When you are looking through the stories in the Bible for an explanation and answer, you must remember one thing: the explanation and answer you receive may not be to your liking. That is not what matters. You make decisions based on knowledge rightly applied, not how you feel. Make sure you are operating in humility and not pride.

God Confirms His Word

As we said earlier, God always confirms His word to you. When you are tuned in to hear His voice, He is constantly leading and directing, confirming what He is saying. He also confirms His Word when the gospel of Jesus Christ is preached. Hebrews 2:3–4 says: "How shall we escape if we neglect so great a salvation, which at first began to be spoken by the Lord, and was confirmed to us by those who heard Him, God also bearing witness both with signs and wonders, with various miracles, and gifts of the Holy Spirit, according to His own will?"

God confirms His Word to bear witness to what He has said. He does this through *signs, wonders, miracles,* and *gifts of the Holy Spirit.*

Signs: In the New Testament, "signs" are associated with "wonders" and "miracles" (Acts 2:22; 2 Corinthians 12:12; Hebrews 2:4). Signs point mainly to the powerful, saving activity of God through the ministry of Jesus and the apostles. The word "signs" is found frequently in John's gospel and point at the deeper, symbolic meaning of Jesus' miracles. The true significance of a sign in the Bible is understood by faith.

Wonders: The Greek word for wonders is teras (Acts 15:12). Wonders denote unusual supernatural manifestations, omens, miraculous events and extraordinary occurrences portending the future.

Miracles: These are historical events or natural phenomena that seem to defy the laws of nature, revealing God through faith at the same time. Miracles are essentially expressions of the salvation and glory of God.

The Gifts of the Holy Spirit: These are a manifestation of the Spirit of God given to the church at a time of need for ministry. Not every believer will operate in the same gifts. The Holy Spirit is the Creator and Giver of the gifts. The nine gifts are listed in 1 Corinthians 12:7–11. The purpose of the gifts is to profit or strengthen the life of the body or church. The gifts of the Holy Spirit are made available to every believer as the Spirit distributes them (1 Corinthians 12:11). They are not meant to be acknowledged in a passive way, but welcomed and anticipated (1 Corinthians 13:1; 1 Corinthians 14:1).

You are now transitioning from the Word of God to the Spirit of God. First comes the Word, then the Spirit. The Spirit of God is *waiting* for the Word of God to be spoken. Genesis 1:1–3 says: "In the beginning God created the heavens and the earth. The earth was without form, and void; and darkness was on the face of the deep. And *the Spirit of God was hovering* over the face of the waters. Then *God said,* 'Let there be light'; *and there was light."*

In the beginning was God (Genesis 1:1). In the beginning was the Word (John 1:1). Notice that the Spirit of God was hovering over the face of the waters. The Spirit of God was waiting for the Word of God to be spoken. When God said, "Let there be light," the Holy Spirit confirmed the Word of God with light. When you speak God's Word in faith, the Holy Spirit will confirm His Word. When God gives you a word, and you hold on to that word in faith, the Lord will confirm His word.

In Words and in Deeds

The kingdom of God is advanced in two ways and two ways only—in words and in deeds. Let's look at Luke 24:19: "He said to them, 'What things?' So they said to Him, 'The things concerning Jesus of Nazareth, who was a Prophet mighty *in deed and word* before God and all the people.'" Then again in Colossians 3:17, we read: "Whatever you do *in word or deed,* do all in the name of the Lord Jesus, giving thanks to God the Father through Him."

God's Word has to come in your life before your life will change. When you accept Jesus as Lord and Savior, you become a new creation. You now have God's enabling power available to you. He desires for you to be mighty in word and deed in this lifetime to fulfill His plan for your life. This requires getting His Word in you. When the Word gets into you, the deeds will follow.

When There Appears to Be No Answer in the Word

Earlier I stated that the Bible has an explanation and answer for every situation in life. So what happens when you can't seem to find the answer you need in God's Word?

David wrote about times like these. "As the deer pants for the water brooks, so pants my soul for You, O God" (Psalm 42:1). These are dry and lonely times in life when only a word directly from the river of God's throne room will satisfy. Let's read Revelation 22:1–2: "He showed me a pure river of water of life, clear as crystal, proceeding from the throne of God and of the Lamb. In the middle of its street, and on either side of the river was the tree of life, which bore twelve fruits, each tree yielding its fruit every month. The leaves of the tree were for the healing of the nations."

God's answer is always in His Word, but you must wait until His Spirit reveals it to you. It can be difficult to wait, but God says to "be still" and trust in His power and faithfulness. You will have His answer when the timing is right. Psalm 46:10 says "Be still, and *know* that I am God; I will be exalted among the nations, I will be exalted in the earth!"

In Step #5, we discussed the following:

- How Jesus is the Word, living and powerful

- How *logos* and *rhema* are illustrated by the sword

- How the Word is your map and the Holy Spirit your compass

- How revelation knowledge through God's Word should become a lifestyle

- How the Word will speak to you directly

- How the principle of identification in the Word operates in the decision-making process

- How God confirms His Word with signs, wonders, miracles, and gifts of the Holy Spirit

- How the kingdom of God is advanced in two ways only: in words and deeds

- How to know what to do when there appears to be no answer in the Word

Categories 1 through 3 deal with natural knowledge. Categories 4 through 6 deal with spiritual knowledge. There are seven questions you have to ask yourself when making a wise decision.

Question #1—What have I learned from personal successes and mistakes?

Question #2—What have I learned from others' successes and mistakes?

Question #3—What have I learned from technical knowledge?

Question #4—What have I learned from wise counsel?

Question #5—What have I learned from the Word of God?

Once you have answered questions 1–5, you are ready to move on to Step #6 in making a wise decision. You are now transitioning from revelation knowledge from the Word of God to revelation knowledge by the Spirit of God. The Spirit of Wisdom is a person. "I love those who love me, and those who seek me diligently will find me" (Proverbs 8:17).

DISCUSSION

1. What is the fifth category of knowledge?

2. What is the difference between the *logos* and the *rhema*?

3. What are the three steps to prosperous living described in Psalm 1:1–3?

    C_____, P_____, M_____.

4. Based on Hebrews 2:3–4, how does God confirm His Word to us?

    S____, W_____, M_____, G____ __ __ ____

    ____

5. True or false:

    •   The Word of God is a book just like any other book.

    •   The Word of God is living and powerful.

    •   God does not communicate with His people supernaturally.

    •   The Bible has the explanation and answer for every situation in life.

- The kingdom of God is advanced in two ways only—words and deeds.

- God gave us examples in the Bible to help us identify and go through life situations.

Step #6: *Learning from the Holy Spirit*

The fear of the Lord is the instruction of wisdom, and before honor is humility.—Proverbs 15:33

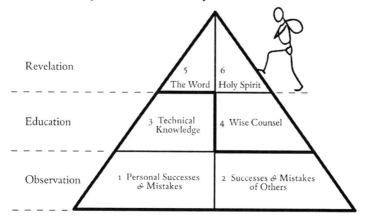

You can talk about the Holy Spirit for hours and only scratch the surface. Entire books have been written about Him. So we will be discussing a very specific part of the Holy Spirit's role in our lives—the revelation knowledge He gives us to help us make good decisions.

The Lord gave me a couple of scriptural definitions of revelation knowledge from the Bible. These definitions are based on Paul's prayers in Ephesians 1 and 3. One of them is *believing, understanding, and experiencing God's person, knowledge, and power by the Holy Spirit.*

GOD IN THREE PERSONS

We all know that God is a trinity. He exists in three persons: Father, Son, and Holy Spirit. All three persons of the Godhead play a role in revelation knowledge. The Father is the *source*. The Son is the *subject*. The Holy Spirit is the *speaker*.

The Father Is the Source

Revelation knowledge comes directly from the throne room of God to the heart of man. God the Father is the source.

God the Father gave His Son Jesus to the world for two reasons: First, to *reveal* Himself to mankind through His Son. We see in Revelation 1:1: "The Revelation of Jesus Christ, *which God gave Him* to show his servants—things which must shortly take place. And He sent and signified it by His angel to His servant John." And then in John 14:9: "Jesus said to him, 'Have I been with you so long, and yet you have not known Me, Philip? *He who has seen Me has seen the Father*, so how can you say, "Show us the Father"?'"

The second reason was to *pay* the penalty for the sin of mankind that you may experience eternal life. John 3:16 says: "God so loved the world that He gave His only begotten Son, that whoever believes in Him should not perish but have everlasting life."

The Son Is the Subject

The overriding theme in the Bible is God's redemptive plan for mankind through His Son, Jesus Christ. Jesus had always been with His Father as we read in John 1:1: "In the beginning was the Word, and the Word was with God, and the Word was God." Jesus the Son willingly paid the penalty for our sins on the cross at Calvary, or as it is also called, Golgotha (meaning "place of a skull") (Matthew 27:33).

It was on Golgotha that Jesus crushed *Satan's skull*—or authority—and his ability to dominate mankind through sin and death. God told Satan this day would come after he caused Adam to sin. "I will put enmity between you and the woman, and between your seed and her Seed; *He shall bruise your head, and you shall bruise His heel*" (Genesis 3:15). That was God the Father's mission for Jesus the Son, and He completed it by giving His life on the cross of Calvary on Golgotha's hill. By doing so, He became the door to eternal salvation. John 10:9 says: "I am the door. If anyone enters by Me, he will be saved, and will go in and out and find pasture." Through His sacrifice, He paid for our sin and bought our redemption, our reconciliation with God the Father.

You *receive* eternal life when you *accept* Jesus' gift of salvation purchased with His life on the cross. The Bible says you are born again, a new creation. God comes to live inside you. You can experience His presence. You have access to God the Father. You can approach Him *directly* for revelation knowledge. John 14:6 says: "Jesus said to him, 'I am the way, the truth, and the life. *No one comes to the Father except through Me.*'" And we read in Ephesians 2:18 how the Holy Spirit, who is the third person of the Trinity, comes into the picture. It is through Jesus the Son that we are made right with the Father, and it is through the Holy Spirit that we are able to gain access to the Father's presence. "*Through Him* we both have access by one Spirit to the Father."

You have to be born again to receive revelation knowledge directly from God. Once a person becomes born again, the floodgates of revelation knowledge are available to every believer. The reason for this is that revelation knowledge is spiritual knowledge. Spiritual knowledge can only be spiritually discerned. "The natural man does not receive *the things of the Spirit of God*, for they are foolishness to him; nor can he know them, because they are spiritually discerned" (1 Corinthians 2:14).

The *things of the Spirit of God* refers to revelation knowledge. All three parts of the Godhead play a role in revelation knowledge. God is the *source*. Jesus is the *subject*. The Holy Spirit is the *speaker*.

The Holy Spirit Is the Speaker

Jesus' last words before He ascended to the Father and sat down at His right hand were the promise of the Holy Spirit in Acts 1:8. His assignment on earth was complete. It was now time for the Holy Spirit and the church age. The church was born when the Holy Spirit came upon the believers in an upper room in Jerusalem as told in Acts 2:1–4.

Jesus came to reveal the Father and pay the penalty for our sins on the cross. The Holy Spirit has come to empower the church to fulfill the Great Commission of taking the gospel to all nations. "However, when He, the Spirit of truth, has come, He will guide you into all truth; for He will not speak on His own authority, but whatever He hears He will *speak*; and He will tell you things to come" (John 16:13). Then in Acts 1:8: "You shall receive power when the Holy Spirit has come upon you; and you shall be witnesses to Me in Jerusalem, and in all Judea and Samaria, and to the end of the earth."

Is the Great Commission part of your equation for seeking revelation knowledge from the Holy Spirit? I pray that it is. You want to get to know the Holy Spirit in order to cooperate with Him. Who is the Holy Spirit to you?

WHO AM I TO YOU, NATHAN?

As I was writing this book I reached a road block at this point. There is so much I could say about the Holy Spirit, I didn't know where to start. I stopped writing for several days, not knowing how to continue. In John 15:5 Jesus said, "I am the vine, you are the branches. . . without Me you can do nothing." That's where I was. For several days I could do nothing without Him. One morning in prayer, the Holy Spirit gave me the words I needed to hear. He asked me a simple question: *Who am I to you?*

Everything I wanted to say started gushing out of me. "You are my Friend, my Teacher, my Counselor, my strength!" Let's see how that revelation lines up with Scripture.

The Holy Spirit is a Christian's *best friend*. Jesus sent Him to you after He ascended into heaven. Jesus made everything He heard from the Father known to us through the Holy Spirit. (See John 15:15.) He is the Helper, the Spirit of truth who speaks truth into your life and testifies of Jesus. "When the Helper comes, whom I shall send to you from the Father, the

Spirit of truth who proceeds from the Father, He will testify of Me" (John 15:26). The Holy Spirit never leaves you nor forsakes you. "He Himself has said, 'I will never leave you nor forsake you'" (Hebrews 13:5). He is always there when you need Him to give you a word in due season. The Holy Spirit loves you unconditionally and will never hurt you or let you down. He sticks closer to you than any earthly brother possibly could. "A man who has friends must himself be friendly, but there is a friend who sticks closer than a brother" (Proverbs 18:24). He is always there to help you in your daily living, ethical, and goal-oriented decisions.

I attended church for a short period of time when I was a little boy. I remember being taught about Jesus and God the Father, but not the Holy Spirit. When I came to Christ as an adult, the Holy Spirit was a virtual stranger to me. Over the years I have grown more in knowledge and experience with the Holy Spirit. He literally became my best friend. I often go to sleep at night telling the Holy Spirit how much I love Him. He means so much to me. I spend a great deal of time meditating on the Holy Spirit and His ministry. I pray you have that kind of vibrant, loving relationship with Him.

The Holy Spirit is the *ultimate teacher*. He is the teacher of the church. He will bring to your remembrance things from the Word and the Spirit when needed. "The Helper, the Holy Spirit, whom the Father will send in My name, He will *teach* you all things, and bring to your remembrance all things that I said to you" (John 14:26). He will impart revelation knowledge to you as you spend time in His presence. There are many teachers of natural knowledge, but there is only *one* teacher of spiritual knowledge and that person is the Holy Spirit. "*Teach* me Your way, O LORD; I will walk in Your truth" (Psalm 86:11). This does not mean that other Christians cannot speak revelation knowledge into your life. Any Christian abiding in the Holy Spirit can impart revelation knowledge to you. The apostles, prophets, evangelists, pastors, and teachers in the Body of Christ are there to equip you for the work of the ministry and to help you grow in the knowledge of Christ. (See Ephesians 4:11–13.) The Holy Spirit, however, can speak revelation knowledge *directly* to you. You need both in decision making.

When I began studying decision making years ago, the Holy Spirit told me, "I will teach you." The Holy Spirit has taught me everything I am sharing with you on decision making. Ask the Holy Spirit to teach you as you pray and study His Word.

The Holy Spirit is every believer's personal counselor! Isaiah 11:1–2 talks about Jesus, the coming Messiah. He is described as a Rod or Branch that will come from Jesse, the father of David. Verse 2 is fascinating in that it describes how the Holy Spirit will rest upon Him. There are six attributes listed describing the Holy Spirit, and they all have something to do with wisdom. One of the six attributes of the Holy Spirit described here is the *Spirit of counsel.* "There shall come forth a Rod from the stem of Jesse, and a Branch shall grow out of his roots. The Spirit of the LORD shall rest upon Him, the Spirit of wisdom and understanding, the *Spirit of counsel* and might, the Spirit of knowledge and of the fear of the LORD" (Isaiah 11:1–2).

I love this scripture because the Holy Spirit is described as the *Spirit of counsel and might*. The counsel, or revelation knowledge, of the Holy Spirit is mighty for helping us make dynamic, God-oriented decisions. He will advise you as you invest time in the Word and with Him. You will readily recognize His voice speaking to you and will be diligent to obey. The Holy Spirit helps you chart the course for your life through His counsel and guidance. Psalm 73:24 says: "You will *guide me in Your counsel*, and afterward receive me to glory."

There are many dramatic stories I could share with you to illustrate how the Holy Spirit has provided me with revelation knowledge and how that knowledge has had eternal consequences. The following concerns a life and death situation that happened to one of my obstetric patients.

I was covering labor and delivery for the day. There were several patients in labor and I was about to perform a cesarean section on one of them. The expectant mother was already in the operating room. She received her spinal anesthesia and was lying on the operating table while we waited for the anesthetic to take effect. In a small percentage of patients, the spinal does not produce the desired anesthetic block, and we quickly realized that was the case with this patient. We decided to repeat the spinal rather than have to put the patient to sleep under general anesthesia, which is riskier for both mother and baby.

While I was in the operating room tending to my patient, another woman became ready to deliver. Since I had my hands full with the first patient, a second obstetrician was paged to care for her. My colleague performed the delivery without complication. The placenta, however, would not come out and the patient developed what is known as a uterine inversion, an obstetrical emergency. The patient was bleeding heavily, as is often the case with this complication.

My colleague moved the bleeding patient to an operating room in the hope of relaxing the uterus under general anesthesia. He made me aware of what was happening, while I continued to tend to my first patient. At one point, I felt a strong prompting to check on my colleague in the operating room next door. I quickly realized that the situation was becoming critical. The patient was now under general anesthesia, but her blood pressure was dangerously low from blood loss and she was close to going into shock. This new mother was bleeding to death before our eyes, and there wasn't much time left.

Realizing that the uterus would have to be manually pushed back into position, I quickly washed my hands, put on gown and gloves, and prayed. The other doctor had already made several attempts with no success. To make matters worse, I had never had a uterine inversion in my career. Fortunately, I was able to get the uterus back into place and returned to my first patient.

That incident impacted me greatly. If I had not been sensitive to the Holy Spirit prompting me to check on my colleague in the other operating room, the bleeding patient would most likely have died.

God is the Alpha and Omega, the Beginning and the End. When He gives you counsel He does so from the perspective of knowing the final outcome. This is where you exercise faith when He tells you something. The next story illustrates this very well.

In March of 2000 I went to Guatemala on a short-term medical mission trip. I was accompanied by another physician, Dr. Perez, and a medical technician named Vivian. Within a few days, we were to link up with the rest of the team in a Guatemala City hotel.

When Sunday morning came, I asked the Lord in prayer about how to find a church service to attend in such a large and unfamiliar city. While Dr. Perez, Vivian, and I were finishing up our breakfast in the hotel restaurant, we heard Spanish praise and worship music coming from a second floor ballroom overlooking the restaurant. I noticed small groups of people going up the stairwell to the ballroom. They were having church right above us! I asked some people, in Spanish, if we could join them and they responded enthusiastically. Little did I know what God had in store.

The large room was full. Some 250 people were present, I learned later. There were about twenty rows of seats with an aisle down the middle. The praise and worship was wonderful. There was a joyful sense of the Holy Spirit's presence in that place. The three of us found seats in the next to last row as the music stopped. Since the message was in Spanish, I sat between my two friends, quietly translating for them.

The associate pastor announced that it was time for tithes and offerings to be received, and a young woman walked down the middle aisle with a small six-by-ten-inch wicker basket. She passed the basket from left to right collecting the offering. By the time she approached us, the basket was full. I thought to myself, *Their offering baskets are too small.* I put a twenty-quetzal bill in the small container with difficulty. The pastor received the offering and everyone prayed. The Holy Spirit then spoke to me saying, *"I want you to tell them their offering baskets are too small."*

I could hardly believe what I was hearing inside me! I was new at this sort of thing. My mind and heart were racing. Surely God would not be asking me to say something like this to a congregation of total strangers! Another thought occurred to me. *This can't be God! It has to be the devil trying to disrupt the service!* But I knew better. Then I heard the voice speak to me again, this time slower and more emphatically, *"I want you to tell them that their offering baskets are too small."* I then reasoned there would be no way in the course of the service for me to tell them. *I'm safe*, I thought to myself. The senior pastor then asked, "Does anybody have a word from the Lord?"

There was total silence as everyone waited. I knew if I didn't act now I would be in disobedience. As I stood up and walked down the middle aisle toward the senior pastor, I could see a concerned look in his eyes. I didn't blame him. He had never seen me before. He didn't know what I might say. I told the pastor I was an American physician born in Guatemala and that I had a word from the Lord. The pastor handed over the microphone.

I shared with the congregation about our small team, the medical campaign, and how we arrived at the church service. They really enjoyed the testimony. I then said that the Lord had instructed me to tell them their offering baskets were too small.

A woman in the front row, whom I later learned was the senior pastor's wife, burst out laughing. I told them that God said to make their baskets big, with faith, according to Hebrews 11:1, which says: "Faith is the substance of things hoped for, the evidence of things not seen."

As I returned to my seat, a woman stood and confirmed the word I had spoken. I knew the Holy Spirit had orchestrated the whole thing.

I received an e-mail three months later from the pastors, Marco and Raiza. They had replaced the little wicker basket with huge offering baskets. The first offering they received with the large baskets was three times bigger than any offering ever! The church had outgrown its current facility and needed a bigger place, and finances, to expand. God wanted to take that church to another level. He needed someone who would hear His counsel and obey.

You don't always understand what God is doing because you don't always see what He sees. He has a higher perspective. This is where faith comes in. One thing is for sure: the Lord's counsel will stand.

The Holy Spirit is your strength. Paul's prayer in Ephesians chapter 3 is for the church to have a revelation of Jesus Christ. Jesus is at the heart of revelation knowledge. The passage starts with Paul praying for the church to be strengthened with might through the Holy Spirit. Remember, revelation knowledge is not just gaining God's knowledge. It is also experiencing God's power, His *strength*. To grow in God's knowledge and power is to be filled with all the fullness of God. Let's look at that prayer in Ephesians 3:14–19:

> *For this reason I bow my knees to the Father of our Lord Jesus Christ, from whom the whole family in heaven and earth is named, that He would grant you, according to the riches of His glory, to be strengthened with might through His Spirit in the inner man, that Christ may dwell in your hearts through faith; that you, being rooted and grounded in love, may be able to comprehend with all the saints what is the width and length and depth and height—to know the love of Christ which passes knowledge; that you may filled with all the fullness of God.*

REVELATION OF GOD'S POWER

There are two ways in which you can experience God's power:

1. The gifts of the Holy Spirit

2. The anointing of the Holy Spirit

I believe most people want to make good decisions. And the reason is simple: they want to succeed in life. Did you play competitive sports or some other competitive activity in high school? I played basketball, and I didn't like losing after preparing all week. Nobody likes to lose. God designed you to win in life. Good decision making *enables* you to do that.

It's probable that those of you reading this book come from diverse backgrounds. Perhaps you have never read a Bible before. Perhaps you come from a denominational Christian background and some of the things I've shared are familiar.

Teaching about the gifts and anointing of the Holy Spirit will be new to some. Perhaps you come from a charismatic, word of faith background and have had significant teaching on the Holy Spirit. I believe the Lord has something for everyone through what will be shared next. I recommend Lester Sumrall's *The Gifts and Ministries of the Holy Spirit* for further study. There are other good books out there. You never stop learning.

God intends for the gifts and anointing of the Holy Spirit to be part of every person's decision-making process. Why is this? Let me take you back to the Lord's definition of wisdom from Proverbs 15:31–33. In order to operate in wisdom God's way you have to know how He defines wisdom. *Wisdom is a range of acquired knowledge that is rightly applied.* Learning from the Holy Spirit is the last category in the *range of acquired knowledge* for operating in wisdom. The gifts and anointing of the Holy Spirit are part of learning from the Holy Spirit. Operating in the gifts and anointing of the Holy Spirit is for every believer.

The Gifts of the Holy Spirit

You know the Holy Spirit is speaking when God confirms His Word. Hebrews 2:3–4 tells us that the Lord confirms His Word to us in four ways: signs, wonders, miracles, and *gifts of the Holy Spirit.*

> *How shall we escape if we neglect so great a salvation, which at the first began to be spoken by the Lord, and was confirmed to us by those who heard Him, God also bearing witness both with signs and wonders, with various miracles, and **gifts of the Holy Spirit**, according to His own will?*

The gifts of the Spirit are manifestations of the Spirit of God for accomplishing His will. They are for the profit of all, distributed to believers as the Holy Spirit wills. Operating in the gifts of the Spirit does not make you more of a Christian than the next person. Christians are to desire spiritual gifts. (See 1 Corinthians 14:1.) Paul teaches on the gifts of the Spirit in 1 Corinthians chapters 12–14. In chapter 13 Paul emphasizes that the gifts are designed to operate by love. There are nine gifts of the Holy Spirit. These nine gifts can be divided into groups of three (1 Corinthians 12:4–11).

The Revelation Gifts	The Power Gifts	The Inspiration Gifts
Word of wisdom	Faith	Prophecy
Word of knowledge	Gifts of healings	Different kinds of
Discerning of spirits	Working of miracles	tongues
		Interpretation of tongues

What follows is taken directly from 1 Corinthians. We have taken the liberty to format it differently so you can better see how the nine gifts are listed.

There are diversities of gifts, but the same Spirit. There are differences of ministries, but the same Lord. And there are diversities of activities, but it is the same God who works all in all. But the manifestation of the Spirit is given to each one for the profit of all:

1. for to one is given the **word of wisdom** through the Spirit,

2. to another the **word of knowledge** through the same Spirit,

3. to another **faith** by the same Spirit,

4. to another **gifts of healings** by the same Spirit,

5. to another the **working of miracles,**

6. to another **prophecy,**

7. to another **discerning of spirits,**

8. to another **different kinds of tongues,**

9. to another the **interpretation of tongues.**

But one and the same Spirit works all these things, distributing to each one individually as He wills.

The gifts of the Spirit can be seen in both the Old and New Testaments. Different kinds of tongues and interpretation of tongues, however, are unique to the New Testament church. The term *prophecy* used in the Old Testament is synonymous with *word of wisdom* in the New Testament. The term *prophecy* in the New Testament is characterized by speaking edification, exhortation, and comfort. (See 1 Corinthians 14:3.) We are to desire spiritual gifts. (See 1 Corinthians 14:1.)

The gifts of the Holy Spirit are powerful and effective manifestations of the Spirit of God for accomplishing His purposes. They are for every believer as the Holy Spirit wills. It is beyond the scope of this book to teach in depth on the gifts of the Spirit, but we will look at some examples of the revelation and power gifts in the Bible. Sometimes more than one gift will be in operation at a given time. For example, faith and gifts of healings may be operating together. Sometimes faith and working of miracles may be manifesting together. The important thing is to recognize the power of the Holy Spirit at work.

Examples of the Revelation and Power Gifts

Word of Wisdom . . . . Scripture

God tells Adam and Eve about the coming Messiah. . . . . Genesis 3:15

David foresees the Messiah will be resurrected from the dead. . . . . . Psalm 16:10

David foresees how the Messiah will suffer. . . . . Psalm 22:1,7–8,16,18

Isaiah predicts a ruler named Cyrus will help rebuild temple. . . . . Isaiah 44:28

Paul receives a vision calling him to preach in Macedonia. . . . . Acts 16:9–10

Word of Knowledge . . . . Scripture

Elisha knows Gehazi has taken silver and clothing from Naaman. . . . . 2 Kings 5:20–27

Samuel informs Saul that his lost donkeys have been found. . . . . 1 Samuel 9:20

Mary knows her cousin Elizabeth is six months pregnant. . . . . Luke 1:36

Ananias knows Saul is blind and he is to go pray for him. . . . . Acts 9:10-19

Jesus tells Samaritan woman at Jacob's well her past.. . . . . John 4:4-18

Gifts of Healings . . . . Scripture

Elisha heals Naaman of leprosy. . . . . 2 Kings 5:1–19

Jesus heals ear that has been cut off servant of high priest. . . . . Luke 22:49–51

Jesus heals a man blind from birth. . . . . John 9:1–7

Peter heals lame man at the Beautiful Gate. . . . . Acts 3:1–11

Ananias heals Saul of blindness. . . . . Acts 9:10–19

Working of Miracles. . . . . Scripture

Joshua causes the sun to stand still for a day. . . . . Joshua 10:12–14

Elijah and Elisha divide the Jordan river on separate occasions. . . . . . . 2 Kings 2:1–14

Elisha temporarily blinds the Syrian army. . . . . 2 Kings 6:18–23

Jesus feeds 5,000 with five loaves and two fish. . . . . Mathew 14:13–21

Peter walks on water with Jesus. . . . . Mathew 14:22–33

THE GIFTS OF THE HOLY SPIRIT IN MY LIFE

In the course of my Christian life, I have experienced all the gifts of the Holy Spirit. The gift that I operate in most naturally is the word of knowledge. I believe the reason for this may be the fact that I am a physician. As a medical doctor I diagnose people's conditions with the intent of helping them get well. For me the word of knowledge is an extension of my practice as a Christian physician. It enables me to better understand what is going on with a patient in order to help him or her. The Holy Spirit manifests Himself in my practice through the word of knowledge on a regular basis.

I shared a story with you earlier about my medical mission trip to Guatemala years ago. There was another incident on that trip that relates to the word of knowledge. Our team treated some fifteen hundred patients a day and held tent services at night. There was an altar call to accept Jesus as Lord at the end of every service. I remember one night walking up to a young man and inviting him to come forward. He was standing with a friend just outside the large tent. It was obvious he wasn't interested in what was going on inside. He kindly declined my invitation. The Holy Spirit then gave me a word of knowledge for him. "You do not want to come forward because you are afraid of what your friends will think. You don't want them to make fun of you, is that right?" He answered in the affirmative. But even though he knew that God was supernaturally trying to get his attention, he still would not heed His voice. I think about that young man on occasion and pray his eyes will be opened before it's too late. It is a sober reminder that the gifts of the

Spirit are for an eternal, God-directed purpose. They are to be handled with respect.

I have had many experiences with the gifts of the Holy Spirit as a Christian physician. The following story is a dramatic example of the gift of faith and working of miracles.

THERE IS NO HEART RATE

Several years ago I worked at a large hospital where I supervised obstetrics and gynecology residents. I received an emergency page to labor and delivery at 8:30 p.m. It had been a quiet day so far and I had spent several hours in prayer and studying the Word. I began praying in the Spirit as I raced to answer the page, and arrived in a large labor room full of people. I soon learned I was dealing with a shoulder dystocia.

A shoulder dystocia is an obstetrical emergency where the baby's head is able to deliver through the birth canal but the rest of the baby cannot. The infant's shoulder becomes trapped behind the maternal pubic bone. The rest of the baby is literally stuck in the birth canal. Special maneuvers are required to reduce the impacted shoulder and deliver the infant. The oxygen supply to the baby through the umbilical cord is compromised during a shoulder dystocia. This is an infrequent but potentially lethal complication for the newborn. There is no accurate way of knowing which patient is going to have a shoulder dystocia at delivery. That's what makes this complication unpredictable and dangerous. Fifty percent of newborns with shoulder dystocia lasting five minutes will die. My page had come at the five-minute mark.

I surveyed the delivery room and saw that the woman on the labor bed had already delivered. A junior resident was attending to her. The senior resident had finally been able to deliver the baby using special maneuvers. The newborn was under a warmer undergoing chest compressions and ventilation through an endotracheal tube.

I was told that the APGAR scores, which measure fetal well-being, were zero. The best possible score is a ten and the worst is a zero, so clearly this infant was in trouble. The room was now filled with pediatric residents and nurses who had been paged once the diagnosis of shoulder dystocia was made.

Despite the seriousness of the situation, I was not fearful when I saw the newborn. I knew God would not let this baby die. I went to check on the mother and make sure she was stable, and then returned to observe the resuscitation efforts on the newborn. I began speaking Psalm 118:17 over the baby: "I shall not die, but live, and declare the works of the LORD."

Five minutes had now elapsed since delivery. I started praying softly in the Spirit. The doctors checked for a fetal heart rate every thirty seconds during resuscitation, and it was always zero. Six minutes passed. Seven minutes passed. Eight minutes passed. Nine minutes passed and the heart rate was still zero.

I asked God, "Why hasn't this baby come back? *Your Word says* if I would pray, this baby would come back to life." God spoke to my spirit to pray with the authority of Jesus Christ, so I began to speak softly, "I command this spirit to return in the name of Jesus," over and over again. This was at nine and a half minutes after birth. Fifteen seconds later, when it was time to check for a pulse, the newborn's heart rate was 100 beats per minute and chest compressions were immediately stopped. I believe the heart beat returned the instant I spoke the name of Jesus.

The newborn was transferred to the neonatal ICU and subsequently extubated several hours later. The baby had sustained a broken arm from the traumatic delivery. There was no evidence of brain damage to the baby despite no heart rate for the first ten minutes after delivery. There were no chest injuries from the resuscitation efforts. The baby weighed more than ten pounds. I went to see him in the nursery the next morning as he was about to start his scheduled feeding.

The shoulder dystocia and resuscitation was an emotional incident for the residents and nurses involved. I debriefed them afterward, commending everyone for their professionalism during a difficult emergency. Several of the nurses prayed routinely for their patients. I took the opportunity to teach them how to pray using the authority of Jesus Christ. My faith grew by leaps and bounds after that event. The incident happened two years after I rededicated my life to the Lord. Jesus brought this dead baby back to life through the Holy Spirit gift of faith and working of miracles.

THE ANOINTING

Hayford's Bible Handbook describes the anointing of the Holy Spirit as follows:

In the New Testament, anointing was frequently used in connection with healing. The Holy Spirit's activities in a believer's life are pictured in terms associated with anointing. Anointing in the New Testament also refers to the anointing of the Holy Spirit, which brings understanding. (See 1 John 2:20, 27.) This anointing is not only for kings, priests, and prophets; it is for everyone who believes in the Lord Jesus Christ. The anointing occurs physically with a substance such as oil, myrrh, or balsam. But this is also a spiritual anointing, as the Holy Spirit anoints a person's heart and mind with the love and truth of God. See how the definition of the anointing is similar to that of revelation knowledge from the Lord? *Believing, understanding, and experiencing God's person, knowledge, and power by the Holy Spirit. Knowing and experiencing God.*

Let's look at 1 John 2:27: "The anointing which you have received from Him abides in you, and you do not need that anyone teach you; but as the same anointing teaches you concerning all things, and is true, and is not a lie, and just as it has taught you, you will abide in Him."

Perhaps you have heard the saying "knowledge is power." Let me give you a slightly different picture: *knowledge and power.* The anointing of the Holy Spirit operating in the life of a believer is knowledge and power. As the definition above explains, the anointing of the Holy Spirit is for everyone who believes in Jesus Christ. I have told you that revelation *knowledge* is supposed to be a way of life for every believer. The *power* of the Holy Spirit through the anointing is also supposed to be a way of life for every believer. Jesus is our example. "God *anointed* Jesus of Nazareth *with the Holy Spirit and with power*, who went about doing good and healing all who were oppressed by the devil, for God was with Him" (Acts 10:38).

Jesus died on the cross so you could have victory in life. He paid the price for you to experience the anointing of the Holy Spirit. The Holy Spirit knows only victory. The devil has no answer for the wisdom and power of the anointing. The anointing is real.

An excellent illustration comes from Mark 5:25–34 and Luke 8:43–48. The story concerns a woman with an issue of blood. You may be familiar with the story. Let's break it down and look at it in detail.

There was a Hebrew woman with heavy and prolonged uterine bleeding. This would be a typical patient in my office. In this case, she had been dealing with this problem for twelve years. Abnormal uterine bleeding commonly starts when a woman is in her mid-thirties. Patients will often see multiple physicians who try different hormonal treatments to correct the problem, to no avail.

"A certain woman had a flow of blood for twelve years, and had suffered many things from many physicians." Notice how the Bible says she suffered many things. I want you to get a picture of the torment this woman lived under. By now she would be in her mid- to late-forties. We know this because the average age of menopause is fifty-one and she is still bleeding heavily.

There are a couple of gynecological conditions associated with abnormal uterine bleeding in this age group. They are called *adenomyosis* and *fibroids*. Both of these conditions can cause moderate to severe uterine enlargement, painful periods, pelvic pressure, and painful intercourse. This condition, if uncorrected, puts a tremendous strain on the sexual relationship between a husband and wife. I have seen men cheat on or leave their wives over this problem. Sometimes the husband will shun his wife. She will try to have sex with him, when possible, even though it may be excruciatingly painful for her. This condition, as the story tells us, often grows worse with time.

"She had spent all that she had and was no better, but rather grew worse." By now this woman had reached the end of her rope. She couldn't just go to her gynecologist's office and schedule a hysterectomy. She had to live with this terrible problem, and the cost had wiped her out financially. Her husband was possibly deceased or out of the picture because of her condition. She was almost certainly anemic and chronically fatigued from the years of prolonged bleeding. And she was most likely a social outcast, chronically depressed, possibly suicidal, from the years of pain and suffering. This woman was financially, physically, and emotionally broken. She desperately needed a miracle! Then she heard about Jesus.

"When she heard about Jesus, she came behind Him in the crowd and touched His garment. For she said, 'If only I may touch His clothes, I shall be made well.'" No one knows where the woman was when she heard about Jesus. She may have simply heard the commotion outside her home as He was passing by and decided to go after Him. She made a desperate effort to touch His clothes, believing He had the power to heal her.

"Immediately the fountain of her blood was dried up, and she felt in her body that she was healed of the affliction." The woman was healed the instant she touched Jesus' garment! Her heavy bleeding stopped and the pain was gone! This was the first time in twelve years she had experienced relief.

"Jesus, immediately knowing in Himself that power had gone out of Him, turned around in the crowd and said, 'Who touched My clothes?'" The woman's faith tapped into the power of God.

"His disciples said to Him, 'You see the multitude thronging You, and You say, "Who touched Me?"'" And He looked around to see who had done this thing. Jesus knew power had gone out of Him. He could see where the power went. Jesus could feel the power and see the power. He had the ability to see His power in the woman who was healed.

"The woman, fearing and trembling, knowing what had happened to her, came and fell down before Him and told Him the whole truth. He said to her, 'Daughter, your faith has made you well. Go in peace, and be healed of your affliction.'" The woman's faith pleased the Lord greatly.

The story of the woman with the issue of blood is found in the Gospels of Matthew, Mark, and Luke. In Mark and Luke's Gospel, Jesus recognizes that *power* had gone out from Him when the woman with the affliction touched His garment. That power the Bible is talking about is the *anointing*. I have felt and seen the anointing as described by Jesus in this story.

After a recent move, I visited a couple of churches in the process of trying to find a church home. In one church, I was introduced to a senior pastor after an evening service. When I shook his right hand, I could see the anointing in the Spirit.

It was as if his right arm was transparent. I could see brilliant, liquid light coming out of the area where his heart would be. The "liquid" was traveling down the center of his arm toward his hand like a cable of liquid light. Not only could I *see* it in my spirit, I could also *feel* it in my spirit as I watched it approaching my right hand. I could feel the power of the anointing leaving the pastor, just like Jesus described power leaving His body. The feeling was similar to water flowing through a hose when opening the valve. You can feel the force of the water flowing before it comes out the end. I watched as the anointing traveled down his arm. Once the anointing reached his hand, I could feel the anointing with my natural hand. The anointing is beautiful.

How did the woman with the issue of blood tap into the anointing of God? The answer is faith. Faith touches the heart of God and releases His anointing in your life. Jesus said so in Mark 5:34. "He said to her, 'Daughter, your faith has made you well.'"

Romans 10:17 says that faith comes by hearing and hearing by the Word of God. Do you want faith that releases the anointing of God in your life? Give the Word of God preeminence in your life. The Lord honors those who honor His Word. Faith will come and the anointing will follow. Many people in the crowd touched Jesus that day, but the anointing went to the person with faith who pressed in to be close to the Lord. Remember James 4:8 says to draw near to God and He will draw near to you. Do you want more of God's anointing in your life? All you need is a hunger to be closer to Him. The anointing of the Holy

Spirit is both His knowledge and His power. The anointing will speak to you and through you.

We have now completed Step #6 in making a wise decision: learning from the Holy Spirit. There are seven questions you have to ask yourself when making a wise decision.

Question #1—What have I learned from personal successes and mistakes?

Question #2—What have I learned from others' successes and mistakes?

Question #3—What have I learned from technical knowledge?

Question #4—What have I learned from wise counsel?

Question #5—What have I learned from the Word of God?

Question #6—What have I learned from the Holy Spirit?

Once you have answered questions #1 through #6 you are ready to move on to Step #7, the last step in making a wise decision. You have gone through the full range of acquired knowledge. Remember, wisdom is a range of acquired knowledge that is *rightly applied*. In step #7 you will learn how to rightly apply your acquired knowledge. Acquired knowledge plus right application equals wisdom.

DISCUSSION

1. What is the third level of knowledge?

2. What are the fifth and sixth categories of knowledge?

3. What are the two scriptural definitions of revelation knowledge from Ephesians chapters 1 and 3?

4. Revelation knowledge is not only experiencing God's k_____, but also His p____.

5. Two ways in which a believer can experience God's power are the g____ of the Holy Spirit and the a_____.

6. True or false:

- Revelation knowledge is experiencing God's knowledge and His power.

- The gifts of the Holy Spirit are for every believer.

- The gifts of the Holy Spirit operate as the Spirit wills.

- The anointing of the Holy Spirit is for only a select few.

- The woman with the issue of blood tapped into Jesus' anointing by her faith.

- The Bible tells us that as you draw near to God, He will draw near to you.

- We draw near to God by faith and a hunger to be closer to Him.

7. Using the biblical decision-making process, what are the six questions you have to ask yourself in making a wise decision?

8. List examples of revelation knowledge God has given you in the past to help you make wise decisions.

STEP #7: THE POINT OF DECISION

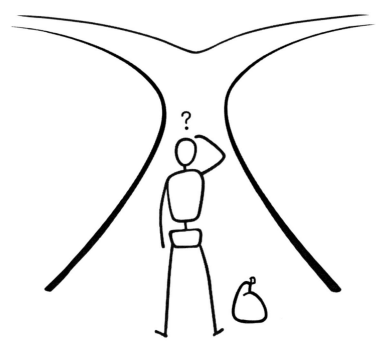

Once you have acquired the necessary knowledge in Steps 1–6, you have planted your feet on top of the mountain, or high hill. Like Samuel, you have now reached the summit. You have all the observation, education, and revelation knowledge needed to make a wise decision. You have reached Step #7, the proverbial "fork in the road where the paths meet." I call this the point of decision. You must now make a decision. But how do you know for certain the decision you are going to make is a wise one? Proverbs 8:1–2 tells us: "*Does not wisdom cry out, and understanding lift up her voice? She takes her stand on the top of the high hill, beside the way where the paths meet.*"

WHAT MAKES A DECISION WISE

Ecclesiastes 12:13–14 says: "Let us hear the conclusion of the whole matter: *Fear God and keep His commandments*, for this is man's all. For God will bring every work into judgment, including every secret thing, whether good or evil." And then we read again in Exodus 20:5–6: "I, the LORD your God, am a jealous God, visiting the iniquity of the fathers upon the children to the third and fourth generations of those who hate Me, but showing mercy to thousands, to those who *love Me and keep My commandments*."

A decision is wise if it is made in *the fear of the Lord* and in *keeping with His commandments*, or written word. These two criteria have to be met for a decision to be wise. The fear of the Lord in the Bible refers to reverential respect and awe. It does not matter if you are making a daily living, ethical, or goal-oriented decision; these are the only two questions left to answer.

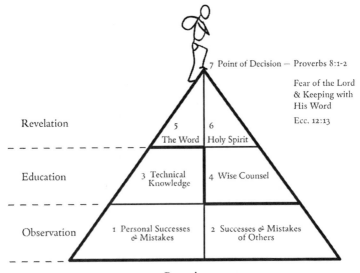

Proverbs 15:31-33

If the answer is "yes" to these two questions, you have made a wise decision. You can rest confidently that you are operating in wisdom. The Lord gave me the example of the litmus paper to illustrate this point. Litmus paper is paper impregnated with litmus and used as a pH indicator. The paper changes color based on the type of solution it comes into contact with, whether acidic or alkaline. The paper will turn red if the solution is acidic, and blue if the solution is alkaline or sweet. Using the fear of the Lord and His Word as your litmus paper will help you avoid poor (acidic) decisions and make wise (sweet) decisions. Keep Psalm 111:10 in mind: "The fear of the LORD is the beginning of wisdom; a good understanding have all those who do His commandments."

Common Pitfalls

It's possible to be convinced in your mind that you're making a right decision and actually be headed toward disaster. Everyone thinks their decisions are right, but the fear of God and His Word are the standard for the decisions we make in life. Even people with good intentions can make foolish choices. The reason for this is that wise decisions are not based on good intentions. Wise decisions are based on a range of acquired knowledge rightly applied, or the biblical decision-making process. "There is a way that seems right to a man, but its end is the way of death" (Proverbs 14:12, 16:25).

In my years of studying decision making, I have observed some common pitfalls people fall into. The following are six of the most common pitfalls:

1. Pr(I)de: the big "I" in the middle

2. Fear: holding on to the boat rail

3. Impatience: you are not at the bridge yet

4. Indecisiveness: sitting on the fence

5. Overanalyzing: analysis paralysis

6. Overwhelmed: Lord, tell me what to do.

Pr(I)de: the big "I" in the middle. Pride has to be dealt with at every step of the decision-making process. Remember the twelve rules of knowledge. Rules 9 and 10 say the following about humility and pride:

9. Humility, like strength, enables you to climb the mountain of knowledge.

10. Pride, like gravity, prevents you from climbing the mountain of knowledge.

In 1 Peter 5:5 we read: "God resists the proud, but gives grace to the humble." God gives grace, the supernatural ability to do what you could not do otherwise, to a humble person. He literally resists, or opposes, a proud person. Many of the struggles people go through in life are the direct result of pride. People don't want to learn from personal experiences or those of others. They don't want to receive technical knowledge or wise counsel from others. They don't want to hear what the Word of God or the Holy Spirit has to say to them. Lastly, they make decisions that are not in the fear of the Lord or in keeping with His Word. The source of this way of thinking is pride. This is worth repeating: *At the root of every poor decision there is an element of pride.*

At the center of the word pride is a big "I." I is the god of self. It is the god of "I don't need anyone to tell me what to do. I am better than anyone else. I can do what I want. I—I—I! In Proverbs 16:18 the Bible says this about pride: "Pride goes before destruction, and a haughty spirit before a fall."

Satan had a haughty spirit and he fell mightily. His fall from heaven was a direct result of pride. If he cannot deceive believers or tempt them to sin, he uses pride as his ace card. Pride is his most dangerous strategy for you and me. Pride always comes before a fall. The book of Isaiah mentions the fall of the devil. Notice how many times Lucifer used the word "I" before he fell from heaven's throne room. We have formatted Isaiah 14:12–15 so that you can better see how many times I is mentioned.

How you are fallen from heaven, O Lucifer, son of the morning! How you are cut down to the ground, you who weakened the nations!

For you have said in your heart:
1. *I will ascend into heaven,*
2. *I will exalt my throne above the stars of God;*
3. *I will also sit on the mount of the congregation on the farthest sides of the north;*
4. *I will ascend above the heights of the clouds,*
5. *I will be like the Most High.*

Yet you shall be brought down to Sheol, to the lowest depths of the Pit.

One of the blessings of the biblical decision-making process is that it forces you to check yourself for pride. Steps 1–7, if followed, will help you root out pride in your life.

Fear: holding on to the boat rail. Before we begin our discussion of fear, let's read Matthew 14:22–29:

> *Immediately Jesus made His disciples get into the boat and go before Him to the other side, while He sent the multitudes away. And when He had sent the multitudes away, He went up on the mountain by Himself to pray. Now when evening came, He was alone there. But the boat was now in the middle of the sea, tossed by the waves, for the wind was contrary. Now in the fourth watch of the night Jesus went to them, walking on the sea. And when the disciples saw Him walking on the sea, they were troubled, saying, "It is a ghost!" And they cried out for fear. But immediately Jesus spoke to them, saying, "Be of good cheer! It is I; do not be afraid." And Peter answered Him and said, "Lord, if it is You, command me to come to You on the water." So He said, "Come." And when Peter had come down out of the boat, he walked on the water to go to Jesus.*

With five small loaves of bread and two fish, Jesus had just fed a great number of men, women, and children. Counting only the men, there were five thousand. He instructed the disciples to get into a boat and cross over to the other side of the Sea of Galilee ahead of Him. Jesus then sent the multitude away and went up onto the mountain where He could be alone and pray. It was late at night when He returned from the mountain.

Meanwhile, His disciples had been battling a strong storm, and they were soaked, tired, hungry, and fearing for their lives.

When they saw Jesus walking toward them on the water, they thought, at first, that He was a ghost and cried out with fear. Don't miss what happens next. The disciples were crying out to God and He was the one standing in front of them! Do you see the irony in this? Sometimes we cry out to God and He is right there with us. Jesus, still walking on the water, identified Himself and told the disciples not to be afraid.

What happened next is very important. When Peter heard his Master's voice, his fear began to dissipate, so much so that he asked Jesus to beckon him to walk out on the water to meet Him. Jesus told him to come and Peter began to get out of the boat. The Bible says that Peter came "down out of the boat" and then "walked on the water to go to Jesus."

After Peter heard Jesus' voice, his faith began to rise. Fear and faith can't exist together. The Bible says in Galatians 5:6 that faith works through love. Peter's love for Jesus was so strong that he wanted to get out of the boat and go to Him in the middle of the storm. He got down out of the boat, standing on the water, still holding on to the boat rail. We do not know how long Peter held on to that rail. It could have been a few seconds or several minutes. As long as he held on to the rail, however, he could still climb back up into the boat. The wind was howling, the waves were raging, the boat was being tossed, his friends were hysterically afraid, and his senses were screaming at him, "Don't do it!" He was still soaked, tired, and hungry, but he was no longer afraid. Why? Because faith works by love. You know the rest of the story. Peter let go of the boat rail and walked on the water toward Jesus. I can picture Jesus quietly encouraging and cheering Peter on, "Come on, Peter, you can do it!" Faith pleases God. (See Hebrews 11:6.)

Sadly, some Christians have a hard time letting go of the boat rail. They love Jesus. They want to do great things for Him. When the rubber meets the road, or the sandal meets the water, fear keeps them holding on to the rail. I will sometimes ask people, "Why was Peter able to get out of the boat?" I usually get the same answer, "Because of his faith." Yes, faith had something to do with it. A better answer would be, "Because of his love." Faith works by love.

People who make decisions out of fear, holding on to the boat rail, don't have a faith problem. They have a love problem. Their revelation of God's love simply isn't strong enough to put down their fear. This doesn't mean they don't love the Lord. It is a matter of degree. The degree of their love for Him in that particular situation simply isn't strong enough to override their natural senses screaming at them to stay in the boat.

As you invest time in God's Word and in His presence, you will not only grow in the knowledge of God, you will grow in the revelation of His love for you. That revelation will enable you to make decisions out of faith working through love, and not out of fear.

I caution people never to neglect the Word of God in their daily lives. If you are too busy for the Word of God, you need to change your priorities before you pay a heavy price. Keep your word, faith, and love level strong. This will keep you from making decisions tainted by fear. If you spend enough time with Jesus, you won't want to stay in the boat or hold on to the rail. You will want to be where He is, walking on the water. "There is no fear in love; but perfect love casts out fear, because fear involves torment. But he who fears has not been made perfect in love" (1 John 4:18).

Impatience: you are not at the bridge yet. Have you ever heard the saying, "I will cross that bridge when I get to it." That person is actually saying, "I will deal with that situation when I arrive at it," or "I will make a decision about that situation when the time comes." Some people try to make a decision before they have arrived at the bridge, or the fork in the road at the top of the hill. The problem with making a decision before you reach the fork in the road is that *you don't know what you are supposed to do until you reach the fork in the road.* Do you remember what happened to Prince Samuel's brother in the story of the King and the Valley? He decided which portion of land he wanted without first climbing to the top of the hill and looking around. He didn't have enough information to make a wise decision.

Trying to make a decision before you reach the bridge, or fork in the road, is a waste of time and mental energy. Don't let impatience sabotage your decision-making process. Remember Hebrews 6:12, which says: "Imitate those who through faith and *patience* inherit the promises."

Indecisiveness: sitting on the fence. Sitting on the fence doing nothing, when you should have done something, is an act of omission. Acts of omission have negative consequences. Do not miss the window of opportunity to do the right thing in your daily living, ethical, and goal-oriented decisions. Proverbs 3:27–28 says: "Do not withhold good from those to whom it is due, when it is in the power of your hand to do so. Do not say to your neighbor, 'Go, and come back, and tomorrow I will give it,' when you have it with you."

The woman with the issue of blood did not sit on the fence. She seized the moment of opportunity to touch the hem of Jesus' garment and was healed. The Syro-Phoenician woman seized the moment when Jesus visited Tyre and Sidon (Matthew 15:21–28, Mark 7:24–30). She would not depart from Him until her demon-possessed daughter was healed. She did not wait for something to happen. She wasn't lukewarm or ambivalent in her decision making. She made it happen by exercising her faith.

Some people are experts at sitting on the fence. They will do anything but make a decision. They are, in actuality, making a decision to do nothing. This is different than purposefully waiting for the right time. Don't waste your life just sitting on the fence. Seize the moment of opportunity when it comes.

Over-analyzing: analysis paralysis. Analysis paralysis is when you have analyzed the situation so much that you don't know what to do. "Anxiety in the heart of a man causes depression, but a good word makes it glad" (Proverbs 12:25). At the heart of analysis paralysis is fear. Second Timothy 1:7 says that God has not given us a spirit of fear, but of power and love and of a *sound mind*. Anxiety is worrying about something that will probably not even come to pass. The Bible says in Philippians 4:6–7 that we should not be anxious about anything: "Be anxious for nothing, but in everything by prayer and supplication, with thanksgiving, let your requests be made known to God; and the peace of God, which surpasses all understanding, will guard your hearts and minds through Christ Jesus."

Some of my patients have anxiety disorders, particularly those who are facing surgery. They overanalyze everything that could possibly go wrong. Sometimes they become so paralyzed with fear over remote possibilities that they decide against the surgery and forfeit the benefits the procedures could bring to their situations.

I am analytical by nature. It can be a great strength, but sometimes I have a hard time turning it off. I have to force myself sometimes to stop going over something again and again. The Lord has helped me greatly in this area. When I make a decision, I follow the seven steps and don't look back. It is wonderful. You do not want to exhaust yourself playing "could have, would have, should have."

Get quiet with the Lord and the Holy Spirit will help guide you into all truth and will tell you things to come. (See John 16:13.) I have one last thought for you. Don't be afraid to make mistakes. Mistakes are a part of life. Wisdom is learning from mistakes and not making them again. God doesn't use perfect people. They don't exist. He uses willing vessels.

Overwhelmed: Lord, tell me what to do. There are times for making your own decisions and there are times for God to tell you what to do. I had a friend with a serious problem who was asking for my medical advice. She was growing in the second level of knowledge. She was seeking technical knowledge and wise counsel. I gave her as much medical information as possible as well as biblical advice. I took her through the three levels of knowledge in order to help her make a decision.

I was glad to hear that she had already done some of these things. The Lord had led her to encouraging scriptures and was also speaking to her by the Holy Spirit. This was a woman of faith. She reached Step #7, the point of decision, but didn't know what to do next. She had all the knowledge to make a wise decision but was divided between two courses of action. She was going to have to make one of the biggest decisions in her life but was not prepared mentally do so on her own. She then surprised me with an excellent question: "Is there anything wrong with asking God to tell me what to do?"

The Bible tells us that Joshua made a foolish peace treaty with the Gibeonites without asking counsel of the Lord. (See Joshua 9:3–27.) God would have told Joshua what to do if only He had been consulted. The Lord often told David whether to attack or not whenever he sought His guidance. In John 5:30 Jesus said: "I do not seek My own will but the will of the Father who sent Me." Jesus did whatever God told Him to do. There is nothing wrong with asking God what you should do.

This does not mean we have to ask God to tell us what to do all the time. I don't have to ask God in the morning whether I should brush my teeth or use deodorant. We are supposed to use some common sense. We are to seek His guidance when we truly need it, and He in turn is faithful to be there for us. There are times in life when we are not in a frame of mind to make the best decision, and we have to defer to someone we can trust, usually a close relative. These should be few and far between. On rare occasions when I had a significant physical challenge, Libby helped me make decisions.

Sometimes people have so much coming at them at once that they are emotionally overwhelmed. It becomes increasingly difficult to think clearly or hear God's voice. This is one of Satan's tactics. A good example of this in the Bible is Job. He was a God-fearing, wealthy man, with a large family and many servants. Job 1:2–3 says: "Seven sons and three daughters were born to him. Also, his possessions were seven thousand sheep, three thousand camels, five hundred yoke of oxen, five hundred female donkeys, and a very large household, so that this man was the greatest of all the people of the East." One day, in a few catastrophic moments, he lost everything except his wife! In that instant, Job was emotionally overwhelmed.

Even though his world was turned upside down, notice what he did next. This is what every person should do when circumstances seem overwhelming. "Job arose, tore his robe, and shaved his head; and he fell to the ground and worshipped" (Job 1:20).

In my home library I have a small sculpture depicting a scene from Luke 2:46–47 where a young Jesus is in the temple sitting in the midst of the teachers of the law, listening and asking them questions. The passage says that all who heard Him were astonished at His understanding and answers. When I'm thinking through a decision, I like to think of Him sitting and talking with me in the same way. Like it says in Isaiah 1:18: "'Come now, and let us reason together,' says the LORD.'"

I have had many prayer times on my knees where I've asked Him to come and reason together with me. I present my case to Him using my understanding of Scripture. He then enlightens me with His infinitely wise perspective. My desire, and need, is to be receptive to what He has to say. I already know what I think. I need a higher perspective. I need His perspective. Getting quiet with God during difficult circumstances is the best thing you can do. Sometimes He will tell me what I should do. Most of the time He shows me a more excellent way of doing things.

There are times when God specifically instructs and directs. There are also times when the Lord gives you the autonomy to make your own decisions. He will give you the knowledge you need to make a wise decision, but He will not override your will. The Lord did not stop Joshua from making a foolish treaty with the Gibeonites.

Good decision making is a partnership with the Lord. He wants you to make wise choices even more than you do. I'm glad when my children make good decisions on their own, and I am glad when I can help them decide what to do. As a father, I enjoy watching my children grow in their ability to make wise choices. God, our heavenly Father, is more interested in the spiritual growth of His children than who gets to decide. He is not trying to control you. He is trying to help you grow. Ask yourself this question, "Am I growing into the image of Christ during my decision-making process?" That is what matters.

We've now covered Step #7: the point of decision. There are now seven questions you have to ask yourself. Then you will be ready to make the wisest decision of all!

Question #1—What have I learned from personal successes and mistakes?

Question #2—What have I learned from others' successes and mistakes?

Question #3—What have I learned from technical knowledge?

Question #4—What have I learned from wise counsel?

Question #5—What have I learned from the Word of God?

Question #6—What have I learned from the Holy Spirit?

Question #7—Is my decision made in the fear of the Lord and in keeping with His Word?

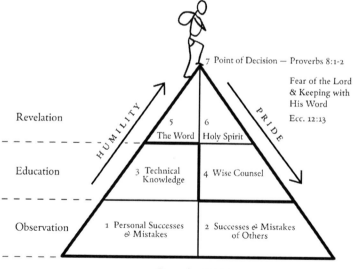

Proverbs 15:31-33

DISCUSSION

1. What is the point of decision?

2. Wisdom = a range of acquired knowledge + r_____
   a_____.

3. What two criteria, or litmus test, determine whether a decision is wise or not?

4. List six common pitfalls in decision making discussed in this chapter. What other pitfalls can you think of?

5. Can you give some examples in your life where you fell into, or avoided, one of the pitfalls in decision making?

6. What is the seventh and final question you have to ask yourself in making a wise decision?

CHAPTER 10

The Wisest Decision of All

During my preparations for writing this book, I listed twenty words I would use for selecting scriptures. Some of the words on the list were *wisdom, wise, counsel, knowledge, revelation,* and *decision.* There were about a thousand verses of scripture containing the words I had selected for study. I wrote down every scripture in composition books, along with anything the Lord spoke to me about a particular verse. I then selected the scriptures for each chapter.

A remarkable thing happened after I made my list of twenty study words. I looked up the word *decision* in Strong's Concordance of the King James Version of the Bible. I was curious to see how many times the word *decision* is found in the Bible. What I saw next surprised me. I discovered the word *decision* is found in only one verse of scripture in the King James translation of the Bible! The Lord uses the word *decision* twice in the same verse for emphasis. The verse of scripture is Joel 3:14 and this is what it says: "Multitudes, multitudes in *the valley of decision:* for the day of the LORD is near in *the valley of decision.*"

The Lord was confirming His Word. He was confirming the parable of the King and the Valley, which He gave me to teach the principles of decision making. The Lord was giving His stamp of approval and mandate to write this book. Then the Lord spoke this word to my heart: *"Son, the whole earth is a valley of decision. And in the center of that valley there is a hill called Calvary. And on that hill there is a cross where My Son, Jesus Christ, died for the sins of mankind. The wisest decision is to make Jesus the Lord of your life today."*

No doubt about it, making Jesus the Lord of your life today is the wisest decision you will ever make. All other decisions in life are secondary. The Bible says that now is the day of salvation. "He says: 'In an acceptable time I have heard you, and in the day of salvation I have helped you.' Behold, now is the accepted time; behold, now is the day of salvation" (2 Corinthians 6:2).

If you would like to make Jesus the Lord of your life today or rededicate your life to Him, I would like to say this simple prayer with you:

Lord Jesus, thank You for dying on the cross for my sins. I ask You to come into my heart and be the Lord of my life. From this day forward, I will live to serve You. Thank You for Your mercy, grace, and Holy Spirit power operating in my life. Your will be done. Amen.

If you said that prayer for the first time, you are now *born again*! It is that simple. Heaven is rejoicing over you. I want to encourage you to obtain a study Bible and get involved in a good Bible-believing church where you can grow. Stay close to Jesus and you will experience the amazing life He intends for you to live!

I hope you have received much benefit from reading this book. My goals for writing *The Art of Decision* were to

- Give you a simple and effective tool in making decisions;

- Help you fulfill your dreams and God's plan for your life;

- Help you walk in victory through life by making wise decisions;

- Restore hope in people's lives that their dreams can come true if they know how to operate in God's principles of wisdom.

My hope is that you, the reader, will see that wisdom is available to anyone who is genuinely searching. I pray that you will know how much God loves you and wants to help you be successful in every area of your life through the principles in this book. I pray you will have a greater desire to know Him more deeply after you read this book. If any of these goals and hopes were achieved as a result of your reading this book, it was a success for me.

For His glory,
Nathan Tillotson

Nathan Tillotson is an OB/GYN physician and surgeon, former military officer, and international speaker. God has gifted him with the ability to simplify and teach biblical principles in a way that is methodical and easy to understand, using great stories and illustrations. Dr. Nathan's desire is to give people practical, biblical strategies for victorious living. He and his wife Libby have three daughters, Katherine, Victoria, and Rebekah.

JUJIPUBLISHING.COM

Teaching * Training * Transforming

To Contact Author

Visit our Web Site: Jujipublishing.com

or

Write:

Dr. Nathan Tillotson

Juji Publishing LLC

8177 S. Harvard Ave. #409

Tulsa, Ok 74137-1600

CPSIA information can be obtained at www.ICGtesting.com

232646LV00005B/54/P